AIRLINE SERVICE ENGLISH

항공서비스영어

Cho, Inhwan · Jung, Hyelyun · Kim, Eunhye · Hwang, Yuri

This book is intended to prepare students for the airline industry. It is based on the real world communication standards for the airline service.

BAEKSAN

Introduction

Purpose of the Book

This book is intended to prepare students for the airline industry. It is based on the real world communication standards for the airline service.
This book can be used in a variety of ways, depending on the needs of the reader:

It can be used as the primary classroom text in emphasizing airline service industry preparation.

It can be used as a supplementary text in a general tourism english course.

It can be used as a tool for individualized study by students preparing for the airline service industry.

What is in the Book

This book contains a variety of situations which airline staff encounters everyday:

Section 1 contains communication standards and handling methods of basic complaints used in the airline service industry. Also, this section provides students with clearly defined steps to overcome difficult situations.

Section 2 contains the situations of in-flight service.

Section 3 contains the situations of airport passenger service.

Section 4 contains the situations of reservation office.

Section 5 contains the situations of ticketing counter.

To the Students

To achieve your goal, students need to work on two areas to improve language skills and service attitudes:

You must work on the airline english.

You must work on the skills and service attitudes on the service industry.

This text can improve your understanding of the airline english and provide the necessary skills to survive in the airline service industry; however, skills and airline english alone will not make you successful. Solid basic knowledge of the english is a must in becoming a successful airline service provider.

Contents

항공용어

Final Destination

Our objectives in the five sections of this text are:

- To understand the Airline English.
- To understand the role of Flight Attendants.
- To understand the role of Airport Service staff.
- To understand the role of Reservation / Ticketing staff.
- To develop communication skills to meet and exceed the needs of English speaking customers.
- To learn Airline Service procedures.
- To learn to manage stress, and overcome difficult situations.
- To be competent and confident in using Airline Service English.

Section 1

COMMUNICATING WITH PASSENGERS

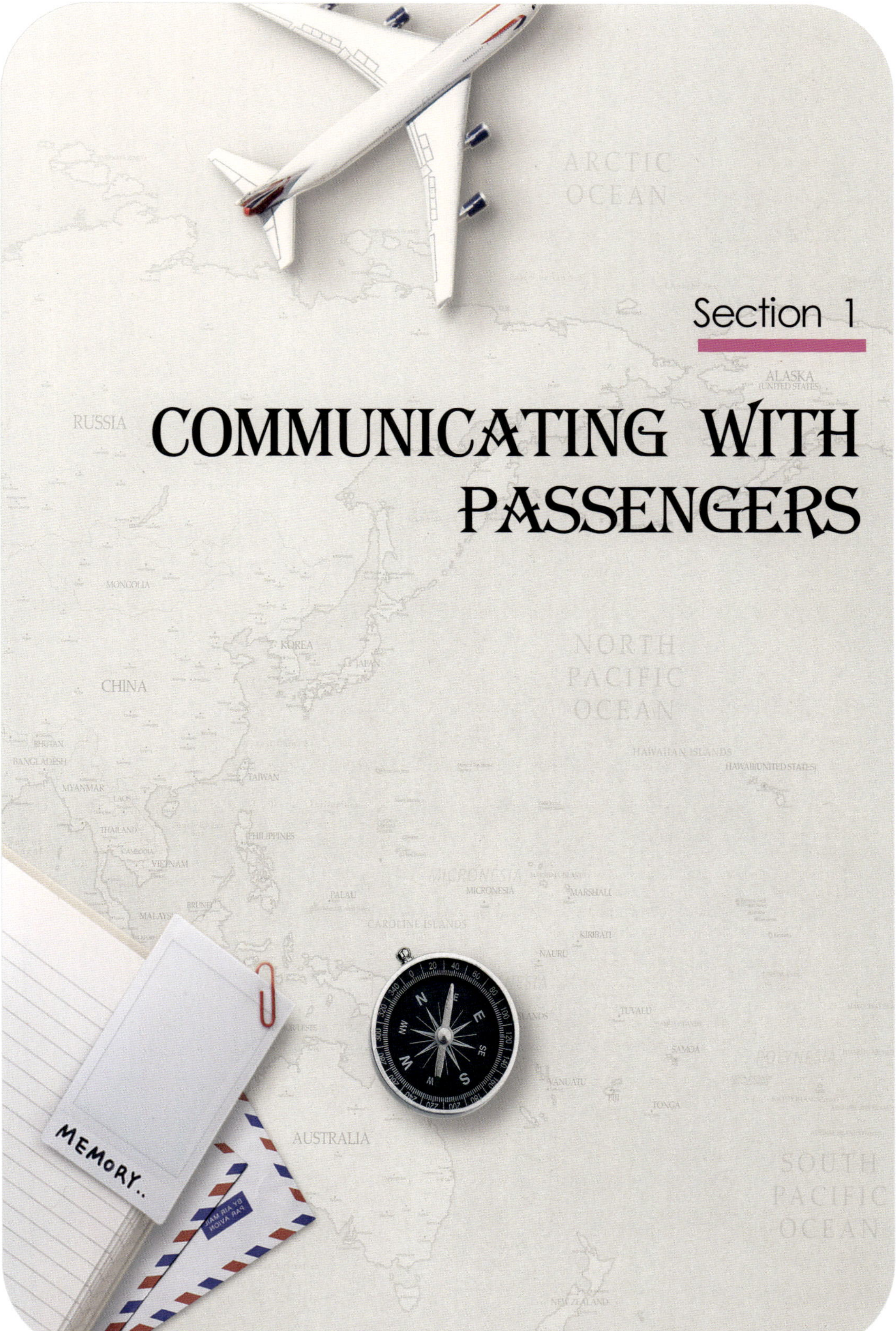

We make our most powerful impression on others when we make them feel as though they are at the center of everything we do ; the focal point of our attention, our concern and our interest. Outstanding service organizations understand this well and use every moment of truth to make passengers feel like special, valued individuals.

1. Active listening

Good listeners make people feel important. Listening is an active process that requires our participation. We show others how actively we are listening through our verbal and non verbal(body language) messages.

Attentive listening

✓ **Give the speaker undivided attention by**

Keeping distractions to a minimum.

Not doing other work.

✓ **Show we are listening to others by**

Making eye contact.

Nodding and saying "Uh huh···, Mm···".

A positive facial expression and facial movements.

Speaking very little.

Facing the speaker square.

Saying "yes" and "I see" ··· etc.

Attentive body language.

Standing up when the passenger approaches.

Participative listening

✓ Check back

Restate details to check for accuracy.

"So that was Flight 18 from Hong Kong on Friday the 25th?"

✓ Clarify

To increase your understanding of a situation or request:

- Ask open-ended questions.

  Could you tell me more about…"

- Restate, using your own words, what you thought you heard.

  "What I understand the situation to be is… Is that right?"

✓ Verify

Summarize the whole message by paraphrasing what the speaker has said. Then give the speaker the opportunity to tell you if what you heard is what was intended.

"Mr. Johnson, what you would like then is information on connecting flights and also on hotels?"

(Note the use of name to personalize the summarizing)

"So you wanted to take it on board with you, but the staff would not let you."

(Verifying to determine if what you heard is correct is a subtle indication to your customer that you are indeed actively listening)

Objective listening

Our ability to listen naturally decreases when someone is angry, critical or upset.

✓ **Do not jump to conclusions.**

Listen to the complete message before making a judgement.

✓ **Avoid threatening questions and statements.**

Put yourself in the customer's shoes and view the situation or request from the customer's point of view.

✓ **Evaluate the message not the sender.**

Be careful not to let your own biases-likes and dislikes-about the customer influence your judgement about the information he or she gives you.

Listening actively to passengers

✓ Give the passenger your undivided attention.

✓ Show you are listening.

✓ Check back details for accuracy.

✓ Ask questions to clarify understanding.

✓ Summarize the whole message.

✓ Listening objectively – don't let emotions, prejudices affect listening.

▪ *Active listening really makes a difference*

- ✓ Active listening makes passengers feel more understood.
- ✓ Active listening enables us to work with passengers to solve problems.
- ✓ Active listening helps us see individuals instead of the same old problem day after day.

2. Questioning techniques

1) *"or" Questions*

✓ **Offer an alternative.**

Would you prefer a window or an aisle seat?

2) *Open questions*

✓ **Person answering gives the new or unknown information.**

- How many passengers will be traveling?
- What day would you like to return?
- Which would you prefer?

✓ **Probing Questions / Gain more information, assess feelings, clarify vague points, encourage people to keep talking.**

- Could you tell me more about that?
- Is there anything else that may have been in your bag?

아시아나항공asiana airlines

1988년 대한민국의 제2민항으로 설립된 아시아나항공은 고운 색동 날개만큼이나 아름다운 미소와 서비스로 고객에게 다가서고 있다. 최근 ATWAir Transport World에서 "올해의 항공사" 상을 수여받는 등 질적, 양적으로 세계 최고 수준의 서비스를 제공하는 항공사로 성장했다. 아시아나항공의 4번째 모델인 한가인 편의 광고 카피인 "떠나세요 더 큰 세상으로"는 항공사를 꿈꾸는 학생들에게 큰 울림이 되는 좋은 카피로 기억된다. 2022년 대한항공과의 통합이 진행되고 있다.

3. Positive body language

✓ Posture

- Staffs should stand with arms relaxed at sides or with hands lightly folded in front.
- When at the counter or computer, you can stand with fingers lightly resting on the counter or keyboard.
- Face the customer(it makes you feel proud and confident).

✓ Eye contact

- With Western passengers, maintain eye-contact. Eye contact shows you are listening, and indicates confidence sincerity and respect. If you avoid eye-contact, the passenger may think you are nervous, unfriendly or are hiding something.
- With Korean passengers, make eye-contact to acknowledge, and lower eyes to show respect.

✓ Smile

Western passengers like smiles / they respond positively to us when we smile. For all passengers, show a bright face and put a smile in your voice.

✓ Responding to difficult questions

When a Western passenger asks a difficult question and you need time to think or want to show the passenger you are taking time to find the best solution, respond verbally "Just a moment, Sir, let me see what I can do for you".

if you cannot fulfill the request, say verbally, "I'm sorry, Mr. Smith. I'm afraid I'm unable to offer you a seat in our first class cabin on this particular flight"

4. The delight of a name

Using a person's name is a powerful tool for the "Service Professional". Use the passenger's name whenever appropriate.

✓ It helps create individual personal service.

✓ It makes people feel recognized and respected.

✓ It helps you appear warm and friendly.

✓ It calms down "excited" people.

With Western passengers, don't hesitate to use the passenger's name.

With Korean passengers, use the name as follow:

- If you know the passenger's job title, use last name and job title.
- If you don't know the passenger's job title, use last name and Sir or Ma'am(선생님).
- If inappropriate to use last name, use Mr. or Ms.(선생님 또는 손님)

루프트한자lufthansa

루프트한자는 1926년 1월 26일 도이치 에어로 로이드deutsche aero lloyd와 융커스 루프트 페어케르junkers luftverkehr AG의 합병으로 설립되었으며, 현재는 유럽 최대 항공사 중 하나로 성장했다. 독일어로 Luft는 하늘을, Hansaor Hanse는 무역동맹을 뜻한다.

5. Handling complaints

1) *Listen*

Do:

- Maintain eye contact.
- Wait until the passenger has finished complaining or explaining the problem.
- Nod and check back(restate, repeat) the complaint to show that you have listened carefully.
- Accept the complaint in a positive manner.

Do not:

- Smile.
- Continue with other work.
- Interrupt.
- Accept responsibility or blame others(other departments, people).
- Justify or try to explain why the problems occurred.
- Argue with the passenger.
- Take the complaint personally.
- Allow your body language to give negative messages.

2) *Apologize and Empathize*

Do:

- Say you are sorry that the problem happened.
- Maintain a sincere tone of voice.

- Show your understanding of how the passenger might feel.
- Keep your apology short and simple.

Apologize:

- I apologize for…(the delay, taking so long to answer your call, etc.)
- I am sorry that…(you have been separated, you have not been given a window seat, etc.)
- I am so sorry that…(you have been inconvenienced, you have been disappointed, etc.)
- I would really like to apologize for…(your inconvenience, the disappointment, etc.)

Empathize:

- I understand…
  …how important this is to you.
  …that this is not what you expected.
  …how annoying / worrying this is for you.
- I do appreciate what this must mean to you.
- I can see that you are… upset / annoyed / worried.
- It must be very inconvenient / annoying, etc.

Do not:

- Justify.
- Sound mechanical.

- Agree that the passenger's complaint is justified.
- Blame the passenger for non-compliance(late arrival at the airport, etc.)

3) *Understand the situation*

Do:

- Ask questions to clarify the situation.
- Ask "WH" questions: when, where, what, who(and how).
- Focus on the problem, not responsibility or blame.
- Restate objectively to confirm your understanding of the situation.

Ask questions:

- May I ask if / for…?
- Could you please tell…. so that I can help you?
- In order to help you, could you please explain ….(what happened, your concern. etc.)?
- Please may I have … so that…?

Do not:

- Ask meaningless questions.
- Make the passenger feel he / she is in court.
- Argue with the customer's opinions.

4) *Give information*

Do:

- Explain any regulations objectively.
- Summarize relevant information.

Do not:

- Justify.
- Talk about your problem.
- Argue with passenger's opinions.

5) *Offer alternative solutions*

Do:

- Decide what you can do to resolve the problem.
- Know company policies / procedures so that you can act immediately(upgrading, compensation, etc.)
- Suggest to the passenger how you can help with the situation.
- Stress the benefits of the best alternative.
- Select alternatives that show the passenger that you are trying to solve the problem. All passengers won't be happy, but they will be satisfied if they feel that you have understood their situation and tried your best to help them.
- May I offer you….
- What I suggest is….
- May I offer the following options….

- The alternatives which are available are….
- To enable you to … what I can do is….
- What I can do for you is ….
- Would you prefer …or…?

Do not:

- Promise anything you cannot deliver.
- Keep solutions "secret".
- Try to avoid the problem.
- Have a negative attitude(view passenger as "enemy").

6) *Gain passenger's agreement*

Do:

- Ask passenger for agreement to action or solution.
- Which of these suggestions / options would you prefer?
- Is this acceptable to you?
- Would you prefer … or …?

Do not:

- Assume the passenger agrees.

7) *Take action*

Do:

- State clearly what will be done.
- Give time / date for completing the action you have promised.

Do not:

- Pass problems to someone else without communicating this to the passenger.

8) *Personalized farewell*

Apologize again. If appropriate, thank passenger for bringing the situation to your attention.

- Once again, I do apologize, Mr. smith.
- If there is anything else I can do, please let me know.
- Please let me know if you need anything.
- Have a pleasant flight / holiday / trip.
- Please let me know if there is anything else I might be able to do for you.

9) *Follow up*

If appropriate:

- Tell the passenger how you are going to follow up.
- Give complete information to others involved.
- Make sure that action is carried out.
- Keep a written record of what you said you would do.

6. Recommendable Expressions

Positive	Negative
I will do my best….	I will try my best….
I will check….	Maybe I can….
I think I can….	Perhaps I can….
May I suggest….?	Maybe you can….
I will check for you….	Perhaps you can….
What I can offer is….	I can only offer….
What I can do is….	You cannot….
What you can do is….	You cannot….
What I can offer is….	It's not possible….
What is possible is….	It's not possible….
Please understand	You must understand….
Difficulties	Problem
Misplaced	Missing / lost
Fully booked	Overbooked
What I can offer is a seat in….	Downgrade
May I recommend….	How about….?
Unfortunately, we are unable to offer… but what we can do is….	The regulations say….
I'll find out….	I don't know….
I'm sorry, perhaps I did not explain this very well….	Didn't you hear the announcement?
I'm sorry, perhaps I did not explain this very well….	I've already said….
I understand….	Yes, yes, yes.(Impatient tone)

항공상식 1

항공기 무게와 균형

어릴 적 시소를 타본 기억은 누구나 가지고 있을 것이다.

한쪽 끝에는 아이가 또 한쪽 끝에는 아버지가 타고 있다면 항상 아버지쪽으로 기울게 되는 시소를 바로잡기 위해 아버지가 앞쪽 자리로 옮겨 앉아 균형을 잡던 풍경도 함께 기억하리라 생각된다. 항공기에도 이러한 원리가 적용되어 있고 이번에 설명할 내용이 바로 이 무게와 균형Weight and Balance이다.

먼저 이 현상을 설명하기 위해서는 모멘트Moment라는 용어를 도입할 필요가 있다. 이 모멘트는 중심점으로부터 떨어진 거리와 그 무게를 곱한 물리량으로 항공기의 무게와 균형을 취급하는 데 기본이 되는 개념이다.

항공기의 경우 중심점Center of Gravity, 통상 C.G라 불림을 기준으로 전방과 후방의 모멘트를 서로 맞추어야만 이륙이 가능한데, 일단 탑승한 승객이나 화물의 무게나 탑승위치를 바꿀 수는 없으므로 전방과 후방의 모멘트를 조절하게 된다.

우스운 예를 한 가지 들어보자. 만일 제주도에 씨름 대회가 있어서 씨름선수 1백명이 B737항공기에 탑승, 이 선수들이 모두 뒤쪽 자리에 앉겠다고 해서 몽땅 맨 뒷 열부터 탑승을 한다면 이 항공기는 중심점이 뒤로 현저하게 움직이게 되므로 항공기가 이륙을 할 때 조종사가 조종간을 당기기 이전에 벌써 꼬리날개가 활주로 표면에 부딪히는 상황이 도래해 결국 이륙을 할 수 없게 된다.

위의 예는 물론 극단적인 경우로서 실제 발생할 가능성은 없지만 항공기의 중심점을 설정, 운영하는 것은 매우 중요한 문제로 중심점이 전방으로 움직일수록 공기역학적 저항이 커져 연료를 더 많이 소모하게 돼 회사의 수익성에 도움이 되지 못하고 심지어 항공기의 운항이 불가능할 수도 있다. 이제 여러분이 공항에서 자리를 받을 때 왜 나만 뒷자리로 혼자 뚝 떨어져 가야 하는가에 대한 불만을 조금 줄일 수 있지 않을까 싶다.

에어프랑스air france

에어프랑스는 탄소배출 및 연료소비를 줄이는 최신 기종을 운영함으로써 글로벌 환경문제 해결에 동참하는 선진항공사로서의 이미지를 고객에게 적극적으로 전달하고 있다.

Section 2

RESERVATION

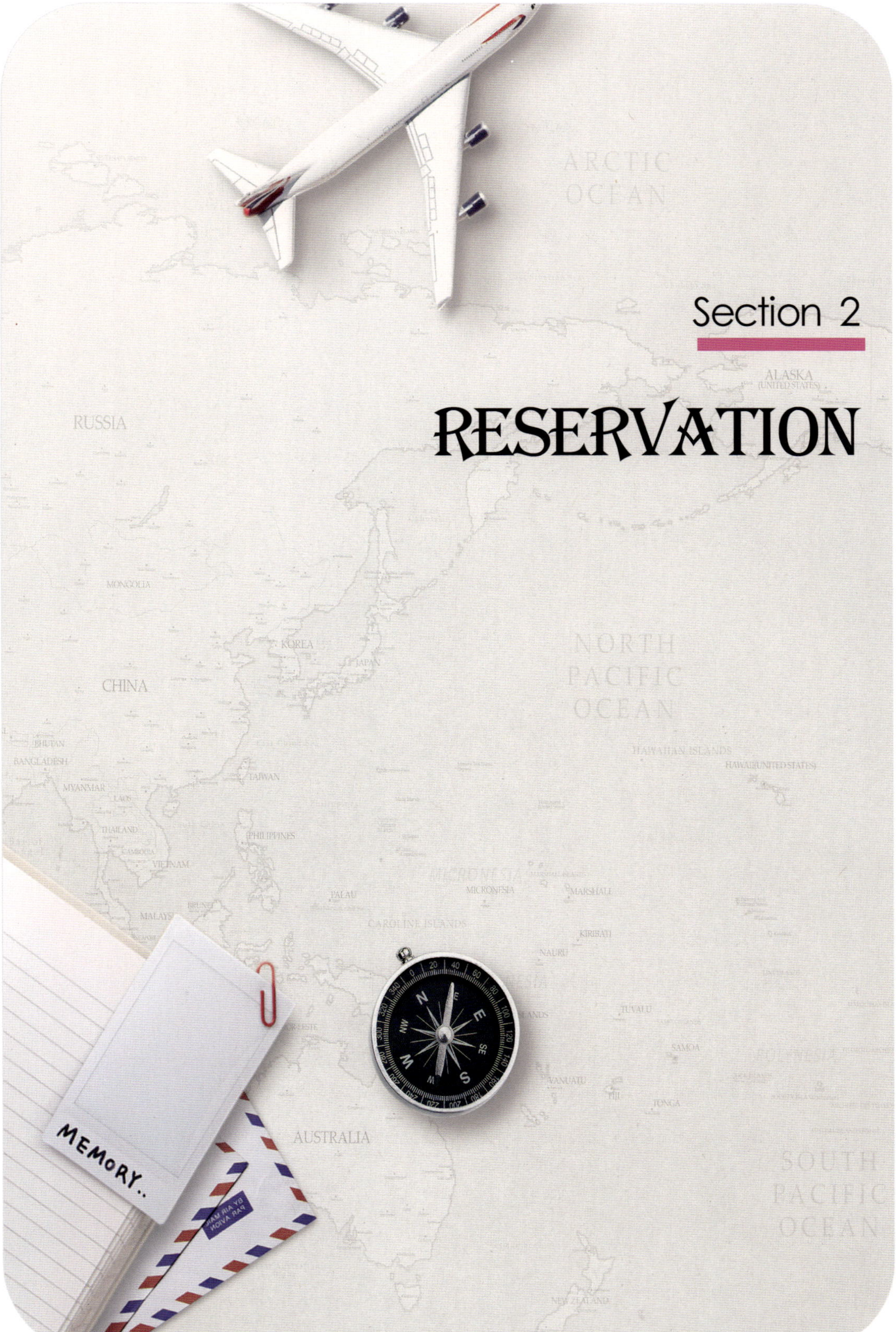

Objectives

To expand your English vocabulary in airline industry.

To role-play various Reservation situations with a focus on appropriate service English.

To practice using polite and positive English to deal with demanding passenger situations.

To discuss real life situations experienced in Reservation office and develop strategies in English to delight customers.

Situation 1 Request a booking

• ***words and phrases***

smile airlines Reservations	How may I help you?
May I have your name?	Window or aisle seat?
First, Business or Economy class?	Smile Airlines flight 10
I'll check that for you now	Business or Residential number?
Thank you for waiting	Flight details
We have seats available	Round trip ticket
I'll book that for you now	Computer reference
May I confirm	smile airlines mileage program
I have reserved	

Mr. Kim: smile airlines Reservations staff | **Ms. Jones**: Customer

Mr. Kim Good morning, smile airlines reservations. This is Mr. Kim speaking. How may I help you?

Ms. Jones Hello, I am phoning to find out about my flights to New York.

Mr. Kim Certainly Ma'am. May I have your name and planned dates of travel?

Ms. Jones Yes, my name is Alice Jones and I would like to fly on July 25.

Mr. Kim Ms. Jones, your name is spelled J-O-N-E-S, initial A. Is that correct?

Ms. Jones Yes that's right.

Mr. Kim Thank you Ms. Jones. I'll check that for you now. Thank you for waiting Ms. Jones. We have seats available in all classes to New York on July 25. How many people will be traveling?

Ms. Jones Just myself.

Mr. Kim And would you like to travel First, Business or Economy class?

Ms. Jones Economy please.

Mr. Kim Would you prefer a window or an aisle seat?

Ms. Jones I'd like a window seat please.

Mr. Kim Certainly Ms. Jones. I'll book that for you now. Thank you for waiting. Ms. Jones, I have booked window seat 36A for you. May I confirm our return booking at this time?

Ms. Jones Yes why not. I plan to return to Seoul on August 10.

Mr. Kim Thank you Ms. Jones. I have confirmed you on Smile Airlines Flight 10 from New York and I have reserved the same window seat 36A for you.

Ms. Jones Oh that's great. Thank you so much.

Mr. Kim You are welcome. May I have a telephone number where you can be contacted Ms. Jones?

Ms. Jones Yes, 290-0405.

Mr. Kim That's 290-0405. And is that a office or residential number?

Ms. Jones Office number.

Mr. Kim Thank you. I'd like to give you your flight details. Do you have a pen handy?

Ms. Jones Yes.

Mr. Kim Ms. Jones, you are confirmed on Smile Airlines flight 18 to New York on July 25 departing Seoul at 10:40AM. You will arrive in New York at 10:20 AM on July 25. Your return flight is on August 10 on Smile Airlines flight 10. I have reserved window seat 36A in Economy class for you both to and from New York. The fare for this round trip ticket is 1,200,000 Won.

I'll also give you your computer reference for this booking in case you want to make any changes. It is G(for golf) 2549 L(for London). Just quote this number and we will be able to help you immediately.

Ms. Jones OK, great.

Mr. Kim Ms. Jones, are you a smile airlines mileage program member?

Ms. Jones Oh yes I am. My number is 2900405.

Mr. Kim That's 2900405. Ms. Jones, will you be able to pick up your ticket by 4:00PM July 12?

Ms. Jones Yes I think so.

Mr. Kim If for any reason you are unable to pick up the

ticket, please let us know and we will make alternative arrangements. We want to be sure your reservation is not released.

Ms. Jones I understand.

Mr. Kim Ms. Jones, the airport is very busy during the summer. To make your trip more relaxing, may I suggest that you check-in at least 2 hours before your departure time? Also for your information, the airport tax is 25,000 won.

Ms. Jones Oh, that's good to know.

Mr. Kim Is there anything else I can help you with Ms. Jones?

Ms. Jones No, that is everything I think.

Mr. Kim Ms. Jones, I hope you enjoy your flight to New York with us. Thank you for choosing Smile Airlines.

Ms. Jones Thank you for your help.

Mr. Kim You are welcome.

Ms. Jones Good bye.

Mr. Kim Good bye.

Situation 2 Traveling with children

• words and phrases

Bassinet	How many people will be traveling?
Formula Is that correct?	Baby food
I have reserved	Child meal
For your information	Hamburgers
Please do not hesitate to call us	Hotdogs You are welcome

Mr. Paik: *smile airlines Reservations staff* | **Mrs. Kent**: *smile airlines Customer*

While creating the PNR(Passenger Name Record), Mr. Paik discovers that Mrs. Kent is traveling with her two children.

Mr. Paik How many people will be traveling Mrs. Kent?

Mrs. Kent There are three of us. Myself and my two children.

Mr. Paik May I ask the names and ages of your children?

Mrs. Kent Yes, Amy is four and John is six months old.

Mr. Paik So that's Amy, A-M-Y and John, J-O-H-N. Is that correct?

Mrs. Kent Yes, that's right.

Mr. Paik Mrs. Kent, if you wish, you may reserve a bassinet for your baby. It is situated in front of your seat. There is no charge for the bassinet. Or you may reserve a separate seat for John. That would cost

50% of the applicable adult fare. Which would you prefer?

Mrs. Kent Please reserve a separate seat for the baby.

Mr. Paik Certainly Mrs. Kent. I'll do that for you now. Thank you for waiting. I have reserved three seats for you in the non-window section, 23 C, D, and E.

Mrs. Kent Yes, fine.

Mr. Paik Mrs. Kent, would you like me to order any formula or baby food for your baby?

Mrs. Kent Oh, no thanks. I'll bring my own.

Mr. Paik We also offer children's meals. Would you like to order one for Amy? We have hamburgers and hotdogs.

Mrs. Kent Oh yes, Amy loves hotdogs.

Mr. Paik Certainly Mrs. Kent I'll book that for you now. For your information, an announcement will be made at the departure gate to enable parents traveling with children to board the aircraft ahead of other passengers.

Mrs. Kent Oh I see.

Mr. Paik Mrs. Kent, please do not hesitate to call us if we can be of any further assistance.

Mrs. Kent Thank you so much Mr. Paik, you have been very helpful.

Mr. Paik You are welcome, Mrs. Kent. Thank you for choosing Smile Airlines. I hope you and your children enjoy your flight. Good bye Mrs. Kent.

Mrs. Kent Good bye.

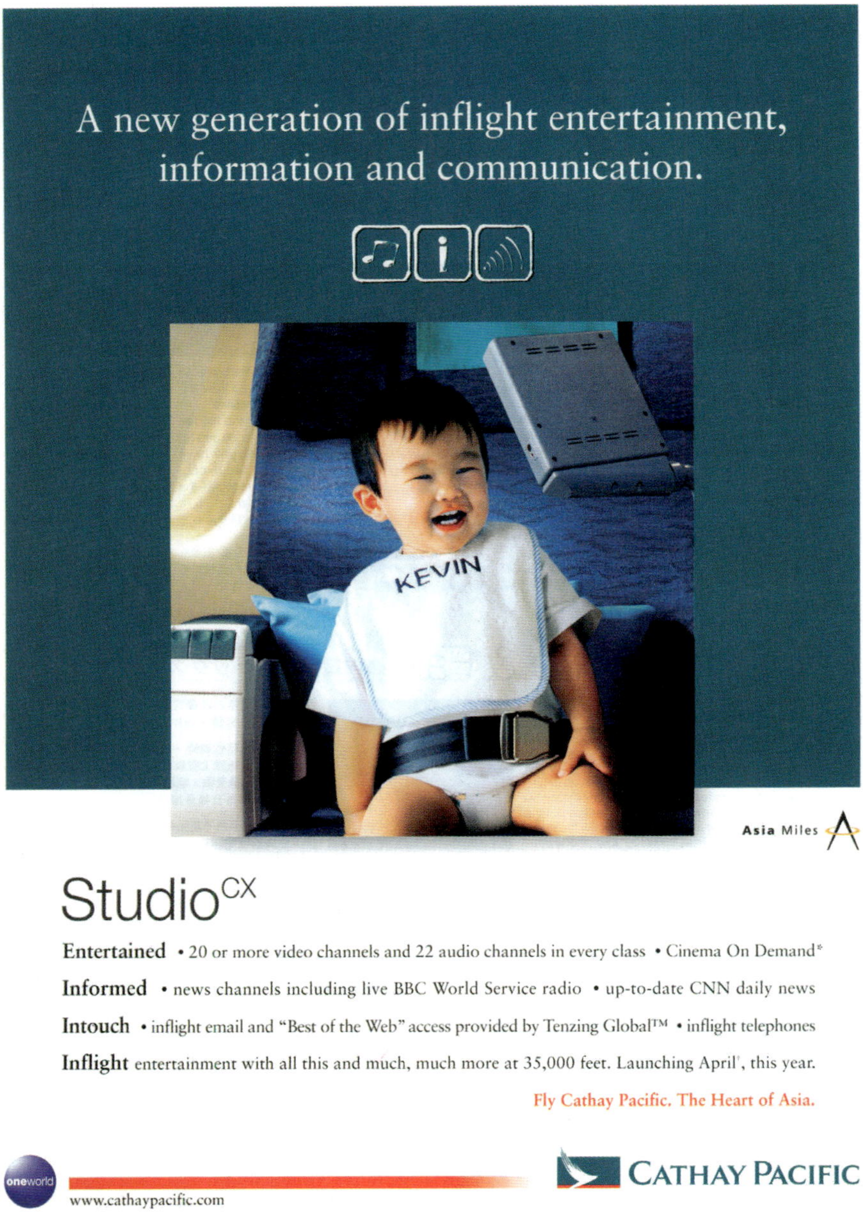

캐세이패시픽항공cathay pacific airways

1946년 9월 24일 미국인 로이 파렐과 호주인 시드니 칸초에 의해 설립된 캐세이패시픽항공은 아시아 경제의 금융 중심도시인 홍콩이라는 지리적 조건과 차별화된 서비스로 세계적인 항공사로 성장했다.

Situation 3 Request a special meal

• *words and phrases*

Vegetarian	Asian, Western, Indian
Meals	Recaps

Mr. Lee: smile airlines Reservations staff | **Mr. Tips**: Customer

Ms. Lee has greeted Mr. Tips and is creating a PNR for his trip to Los Angeles. During the conversation Mr. Tips inquires about special meals.

Ms. Lee Mr. Tips, I have reserved window seat 15A for you.

Mr. Tips Thank you. By the way, I am a vegetarian. Do you offer vegetarian meals on your flights?

Ms. Lee We certainly do. You can have your choice of Asian, Western or Indian style vegetarian meals. Which would you prefer?

Mr. Tips Oh, Asian please.

Ms. Lee Certainly. I will book that for you now.

대한항공korean air

고객들은 개인 프라이버시privacy를 중요시한다. 특히 항공사 비즈니스 클래스 이용 고객들은 비싼 비용을 지불하는 만큼 더욱 개인공간 및 서비스에 민감하다. 광고사진을 보면 옆자리에 누가 앉아도 프라이버시가 보호되고 넓은 공간과 첨단 엔터테인먼트 시스템 등으로 편안하게 목적지까지 갈 수 있다는 점을 잘 보여주고 있다.

Situation 4 Transfer a call to the ticketing counter

• *words and phrases*

smile airlines ticketing office
I am sorry to hear that
They will be happy to assist you
May I have your name please?
I will transfer him

Ms. Wun: smile airlines Reservations staff | **Ms. Lee**: smile airlines Ticketing staff
Mr. Lord: Customer

Ms. Wun Good afternoon, smile airlines Reservations. This is Ms. Wun speaking. How may I help you?

Mr. Lord Hello, I am afraid I have lost my ticket and I am very worried I will not be able to get back to the States this week.

Ms. Wun I am sorry to hear that Sir. Let me transfer you to our ticketing office. They will be happy to assist you. May I have your name please?

Mr. Lord Yes, my name is Frank Lord.

Ms. Wun Thank you Mr. Lord. Please hold the line and I'll transfer your call.

Ms. Lee smile airlines ticketing office. Ms. Lee speaking.

Ms. Wun Hello, Ms. Lee. This is Ms. Wun from Reservations. I have a customer, Mr. Lord on the phone. He has lost his ticket and seems very concerned. I'll

	transfer him through to you now.
Ms. Lee	Hello, Mr. Lord. My name is Ms. Lee, I understand that you have lost your ticket.
Mr. Lord	Yes, that's right....

Ms. Lee finishes the call with Mr. Lord.

Situation 5 Calls for lost luggage

• ***words and phrases***

Lost luggage	I am terribly sorry
May I have you name?	Baggage department
Let me apologize	Contact phone number
Mishandling	

Mr. Lee: *smile airlines Reservations staff* | **Ms. Finch**: Customer

Mr. Lee Good evening, smile airlines Reservations, Mr. Lee speaking. How may I help you?

Ms. Finch Hello, I arrived on last night's flight from Tokyo and my luggage didn't make it. Can you tell me if it has been found?

Mr. Lee I am terribly sorry, ma'am. That will need to be handled by our Baggage Department at the airport.

Ms. Finch Can't you handle this for me?

Mr. Lee I am afraid not. What I can do is take your name and phone number and have one of our baggage staff call you back. Or if you prefer, I can give you the smile airlines baggage office phone number and you can call them directly. Which would be best for you, ma'am?

Ms. Finch Well, please have someone call me.

Mr. Lee Certainly, ma'am. May I have your name and contact phone number?

Ms. Finch Yes, My name is Janice Finch and I am staying at the Hotel Lotte.

Mr. Lee Thank you Ms. Finch, I have the Hotel Lotte phone number here. When is the best time to contact you?

Ms. Finch I will be here until 6:00 this evening.

Mr. Lee Thank you, Ms. Finch. Let me apologize for the mishandling of your bag. I will have a baggage staff contact you this afternoon.

Ms. Finch Fine, I will wait for the call. Good bye.

Mr. Lee Good bye Ms. Finch.

Mr. Lee then follows up by contacting the Baggage Department, explaining the situation and passing the customers name and contact number.

Situation 6 Reconfirmation

• ***words and phrases***

Date of travel	Reconfirm
As you requested	May I confirm

Ms. Park: smile airlines Reservations staff | **Mr. Tan**: Customer

Ms. Park Good morning, smile airlines reservations. This is Ms. Park speaking.

Mr. Tan Yes, I am calling to reconfirm my flight to New York.

Ms. Park Certainly, sir, may I have your name and date of travel please?

Mr. Tan Yes, my name is Arthur Tan and I will leave Seoul on October 11.

Ms. Park And the spelling is T-A-N. Is that correct, Mr. Tan?

Mr. Tan Yes.

Ms. Park Thank you Mr. Tan. I will check that for you now. Thank you for waiting. You will be flying Executive Class on our 8:30AM flight to New York. We have you booked in seat 12A as you requested. May I confirm that your Seoul contact number is 312-0408?

Mr. Tan Yes, that is correct.

Ms. Park Mr. Tan, thank you for calling Smile Airlines. I hope you enjoy your flight to New York.

Mr. Tan Thank you. Good bye.

Ms. Park Thank you Mr. Tan.

핀에어finn air

산타클로스의 나라인 핀란드의 국적 항공사인 finn air는 크리스마스 운항 항공기 동체에 산타클로스 그림을 그려 어린이를 동반한 가족 승객들의 많은 호응을 얻고 있다.

Situation 7 Assigned seat is released

• ***words and phrases***

Difficulty	Reconfirm your flight
Original flight	72 hours before your departure
Message	Seat was released
Fully booked	I do apologize
Expected	
Please accept my apologies on behalf of Smile Airlines	

Ms. Kim: *smile airlines Reservations staff* | **Ms. Grey**: Customer

Ms. Kim Good afternoon, smile airlines reservations. This is Ms. Kim speaking.

Ms. Grey Hi, I'd like to reconfirm my flight for tomorrow to Seattle. My name is Anita Grey.

Ms. Kim Certainly Ms. Grey. And the spelling of your name is G-R-E-Y initial A. Is that correct?

Ms. Grey Yes that's right.

Ms. Kim One moment please Ms. Grey. I'll check that for you now.

Thank you for waiting. Ms. Grey, did you have any difficulty reaching our reservations to reconfirm your flight?

Ms. Grey Well actually, I tried to call last week but the lines were always busy and then I had business outside of Seoul and had trouble getting to a telephone. Why is there a problem?

Ms. Kim I am so sorry Ms. Grey, but because we did not receive reconfirmation 72 hours before your departure, the seat was released. I am afraid the flight is now fully booked.

Ms. Grey Oh, I can't believe this! You people should get more telephone lines. It is just ridiculous!

Ms. Kim I do apologize that you could not reach our reservations department. I understand that you are very concerned. What I can do is waitlist you on your original flight and make a confirmed reservation for you on the following day.

Ms. Grey I am very angry about this.

Ms. Kim I realize that this is not what you expected and I will personally do everything I can, Ms. Grey, to get your waitlist booking confirmed. Will this be acceptable to you Ms. Grey?

Ms. Grey It doesn't look like I have any choice.

Ms. Kim May I please have your Seoul contact number so I can let you know immediately if we get a confirmation on your original flight?

Ms. Grey It is 448-7450. If I am not there, leave a message for me with my secretary.

Ms. Kim I certainly will, Ms. Grey. Once again, please accept my apologies on behalf of Smile Airlines.

Ms. Grey Good bye.

Ms. Kim Good bye Ms. Grey.

Situation 8 Calls for a fare quotation

• ***words and phrases***

Fare quotation	Preferred dates of travel
Special low fare	One way
Round trip	Tentative Booking

Mr. Park: smile airlines Reservations staff | **Mr. Long**: Customer

Mr. Park Good morning, smile airlines reservations. This is Mr. Park speaking.

Mr. Long Is this smile airlines?

Mr. Park Yes, it is. How may I help you?

Mr. Long Oh, I'm thinking about taking a trip to Seattle and I want to know if you have any low fares.

Mr. Park Certainly Sir. May I have your name and preferred dates of travel?

Mr. Long Oh, I don't want to commit myself yet. I'm just checking around.

Mr. Park I do understand. If you tell me when you are planning to travel, I can see if we can offer you a special low fare.

Mr. Long OK. I was thinking about some time in September.

Mr. Park And would that be one way or round trip Sir?

Mr. Long Round trip.

Mr. Park May I ask how long you plan to stay in Seattle before you return to Seoul?

Mr. Long About two weeks I suspect.

Mr. Park Thank you, please wait a moment while I check what fares would be available. Thank you for waiting, sir. The fare would be 1,145,000 won. Would you like me to make a booking for you?

Mr. Long No, no, I'm not ready to commit to a firm date yet.

Mr. Park You are welcome to make a tentative booking now and you can change your dates later if necessary. The flights do fill up quickly and I would not want you to be disappointed.

Mr. Long No, I think I will wait.

Mr. Park Certainly, sir. Thank you for calling Smile Airlines.

Mr. Long Thanks for the information. Good bye.

Mr. Park Good bye, Sir.

제주항공jeju air

2005년 설립 이후 급성장하고 있는 대한민국의 대표 저비용 항공사이다.
제주항공의 광고 모델을 보면 〈별에서 온 그대〉의 김수현, 〈태양의 후예〉의 송중기 등 당대 최고의 한류 스타들을 모델로 내세우는 스타마케팅을 하고 있는 것을 볼 수 있다. 한류스타는 한국과 한류콘텐츠를 좋아하는 외국 여행객들을 유치하는 데 큰 장점이 되고 있다.

Situation 9 Calls for a change in booking

• *words and phrases*

Flight number	Change my booking
Routing	smile airlines flight 22 to Seattle
New schedule	I'm afraid
Fully booked	Don't worry
Via	Jot down
Connect to	May I remind you
To make your trip more relaxing	Before your departure
It is my pleasure	I hope you enjoy your trip

Mr. Kim: *smile airlines* Reservations staff | **Mr. Ross**: Customer

Ms. Kim Good afternoon, smile airlines reservations. This is Ms. Kim. How may I help you?

Mr. Ross Hello, I was originally booked on a flight to Washington for next Wednesday, but I need to fly one day earlier. Is it possible to change my booking?

Ms. Kim Certainly Sir. May I have your name and flight number please?

Mr. Ross Yes, my name is Ross, Doug Ross. I was booked on smile airlines flight 22 to Seattle and then flight 8 to Washington.

Ms. Kim Mr. D. Ross. R-O-S-S. Is that correct?

Mr. Ross That's it.

Ms. Kim Let me see if the Tuesday, February 9 flights to Washington are available.

Thank you for waiting, Mr. Ross. I'm afraid the February 9 flight to Washington is fully booked.

Mr. Ross Oh darn, I really need to get there a day early.

Ms. Kim Don't worry Mr. Ross. I have checked another routing for you and we do have seats available on another flight to Washington which goes via Los Angeles. It departs one hour earlier than your original flight and arrives in Washington at 4:50PM. Would you like me to make the change right now?

Mr. Ross Oh yes please. That's great.

Ms. Kim Mr. Ross, would you like to jot down your new schedule?

Mr. Ross Yes, I have a pen right here.

Ms. Kim Fine. You are booked on smile airlines flight 20 departing Seoul at 10:25AM, and arriving in Los Angeles at 9:00AM. You will connect to smile airlines 17 departing Los Angeles at 11:30AM and arriving in Washington at 4:20PM. Would you like to keep the same seat assignment Mr. Ross?

Mr. Ross Yes, if possible.

Ms. Kim Fine, I have you booked in seat 12A in Business Class. May I remind you that the airport is very busy at this time. So, to make your trip more relaxing, please check in no later than an hour and a half before your departure time.

Mr. Ross Yes, I understand. And thank you for your help.

Ms. Kim It is my pleasure. Thank you for flying Smile Airlines. I hope you enjoy your trip to Washington, Mr. Ross.

Mr. Ross Good bye.

Ms. Kim Good bye Mr. Ross.

항공상식 2

항공기 타이어 가격은?

대개 비행기는 수만 개의 부품으로 이루어져 있고 그 부품들이 저마다 비행에 있어 중요한 역할을 하지만 타이어의 경우는 약간 성격이 다르다. 타이어는 비행 자체를 위해 있는 것이 아니고, 이륙과 착륙을 위해 필요한 것이기 때문이다.

자동차 타이어와 비교했을 때 B747 항공기 정도의 크기라면 그 타이어의 직경이 커다란 현관 문 크기 정도는 돼야겠지만, 항공기 타이어의 실제 높이는 초등학생의 키 정도인 약 1백 20cm에 불과하다.

승객과 화물을 가득 실은 B747-400 항공기의 무게가 3백80여 톤에 달하니 자동차와 비교하면 수백 배가 넘는 무게와 충격을 상대적으로 작은 크기의 타이어로 감당해 내는 셈이다. 일례로, A330 항공기는 타이어 하나가 31톤의 무게를 견디고 시속 4백25km에서도 안전하게 주행할 수 있도록 설계돼 있다. 때문에 타이어에 공기를 주입할 때도 자동차의 경우 그 내부 압력이 30psi압력의 단위 정도에 비해 항공기는 약 7배에 해당하는 2백psi 정도로 유지해야 한다. 그럼 항공기 타이어 하나의 가격은 얼마나 할까? 결론부터 말하자면 매우 비싸다. 항공기 타이어는 자동차용에 비해 소량 생산되는 데다가 앞에서 말한 것처럼 엄청난 무게와 빠른 속도에 대응해 기능과 강도를 유지할 수 있도록 특수하게 설계, 제작되기 때문이다.

물론 항공기 종류별로 장착되는 타이어도 다르고 가격도 다양하지만, 통상 타이어 1개당 값은 1백만~1백50만 원, 여기에 알루미늄 휠 가격대당 약 1만 달러을 포함하면 1개당 약 1천 3백만 원 정도가 된다. B747 항공기의 경우 주 타이어가 동체에 4개씩 4조로 구성되어 있고, 동체 앞쪽Nose에 2개가 더 있으니 이들 타이어 및 휠 가격을 전부 합치면 총 1억 8천만 원 정도가 되는 셈이다.

이처럼 항공기 타이어의 가격이 워낙 비싼 까닭에 설계 단계부터 재생을 고려해 만들어진다. 따라서 규정치만큼 마모된 타이어는 즉시 타이어 제작사로 보내 재생을 하게 되는데 재생과정 역시 엄격한 시험을 거쳐 이루어지며 통상 한 번에 40~60만 원 정도의 비용이 소요된다.

아시아나항공asiana airlines

아시아나항공은 영국의 항공서비스 평가 기관인 스카이 트랙스Sky trax가 선정한 5 스타 항공사로서 아름다운 미소와 서비스로 고객에게 다가서고 있다.

최근 아시아나항공은 취항목적지인 동남아시아 국가에서 많은 사회봉사를 하고 있다. 베트남에서의 사랑의 집짓기 봉사 활동을 주제로 한 광고는 아시아나항공의 따뜻하고 세심한 서비스 그리고 친사회적 기업이라는 점을 고객에게 어필하고 있다.

Section 3

TICKETING COUNTER

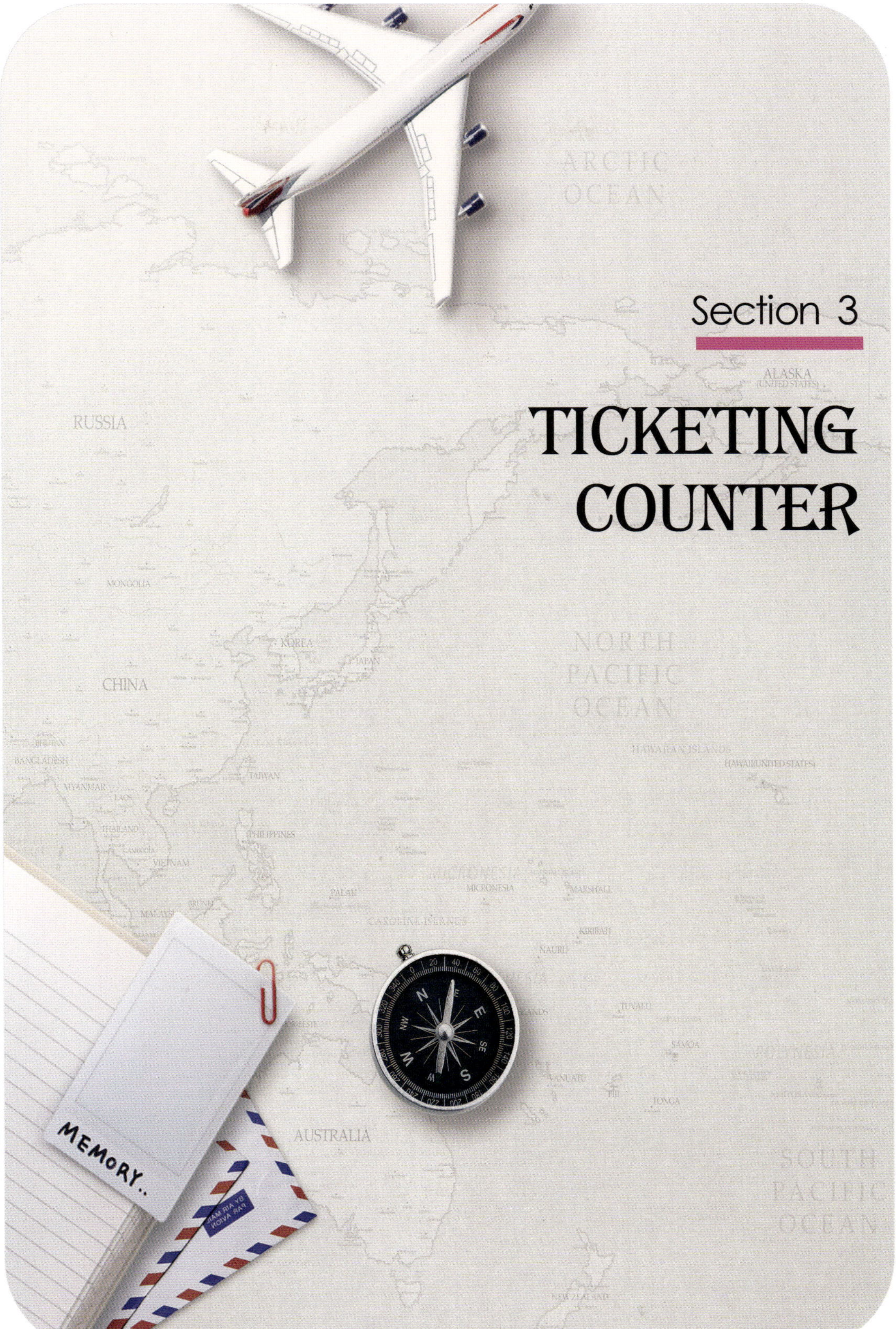

Objectives

To expand your English vocabulary in airline service industry.

To role-play various Ticketing situations with a focus on appropriate service English.

To practice using polite and positive English to deal with demanding passenger situations.

To discuss real life situations experienced in Ticketing and develop strategies in English to delight customers.

Situation 1 Visiting the ticketing counter

• ***words and phrases***

Return booking	Thank you for waiting
smile airlines mileage program	Open ticket
Mileage credited	Very full
ID card	Unfortunately
Ground staff	Review your itinerary

Ms. Park: smile airlines Ticketing staff | **Ms. Lamb**: Customer

Ms. Park May I help you?

Ms. Lamb Yes, thank you.

Ms. Park Good afternoon and thank you for waiting. My name is Ms. Park. How may I help you?

Ms. Lamb I'd like to make a return booking to Detroit. I have an open ticket for a year and I think I'm getting close to the deadline.

Ms. Park Oh, I see. May I see your ticket please.
Thank you, Ms. Lamb. I see that the deadline for using this ticket is March 11 which is ten days from now. On which day would you like to reserve a flight to Detroit?

Ms. Lamb Well, I suppose next week sometime, say the 8th or 9th?

Ms. Park Certainly, Ms. Lamb. Let me check those dates for you now.

Thank you for waiting. The flights are very full but I have two options for you. Seats to Detroit are available via Seattle on March 8 and via Los Angeles on March 9. The flight via Los Angeles leaves an hour earlier. Which would you prefer, Ms. Lamb?

Ms. Lamb Oh, I have an aunt in Seattle so book me on that flight. I can give her a call from the airport on my way through.

Ms. Park Certainly. Would you like me to make a seat selection for you now as well?

Ms. Lamb Yes, if you could.

Ms. Park Certainly. Would you prefer a window or an aisle seat.

Ms. Lamb An aisle seat please.

Ms. Park I'll just check that for you now.

Thank you for waiting, Ms. Lamb. I will reserve seat 8C for you. May I have a contact number for you in Seoul, please?

Ms. Lamb Yes, it is 312-0408.

Ms. Park And is that an office or residential number?

Ms. Lamb Residential number.

Ms. Park Thank you. Ms. Lamb, are you a smile airlines

mileage club member?

Ms. Lamb Oh yes I am, but I have forgotten my card in my other bag.

Ms. Park Don't worry. To get your mileage credited, just call smile airlines reservations at 290-0405. Or you can give your smile airlines mileage club ID card to our ground staff when you check in for your flight.

Ms. Lamb Terrific.

Ms. Park Ms. Lamb, let me review your itinerary with you. You are booked on Smile Airlines flight 21 from Seoul to Seattle on March 8 departing Seoul at 4:35PM. From Seattle to Detroit you are booked on smile airlines flight 8. I have reserved seat 28C for you. Here is your ticket and itinerary.

Ms. Lamb Thank you.

Ms. Park As the airport is very busy at this time of year, may I ask you to check in at least 2 hours before your departure time?

Ms. Lamb OK

Ms. Park Ms. Lamb, is there anything else I can do for you today?

Ms. Lamb No, I think that is everything.

Ms. Park Thank you for choosing Smile Airlines Ms. Lamb. I do hope you enjoy your flight.

말레이시아항공malaysia Airlines

1947년 쌍발 항공기로 항공운송에 첫발을 내디딘 말레이시아항공은 "안전 제일주의"라는 슬로건을 내걸고 안전운항에 역량을 집중하고 있다. 이와 같은 노력으로 최근 국제항공승객협회IAPA에서 선정한 세계에서 가장 안전한 15대 항공사에 선정되는 영예를 안기도 했다.

Situation 2 Ticket sales

• *words and phrases*

Destination	I'm sorry to have kept you waiting.
Credit Card	Preferred dates of travel
Signature	Do you require additional seats?
Receipt	How would you like to pay?
Airport tax	Process
To make your trip more relaxing	

Mr. Park: smile airlines Ticketing staff | **Mr. Jones**: Customer

Mr. Park May I help you please?
Good afternoon. My name is Mr. Park. I'm sorry to have kept you waiting.

Mr. Jones Yes, you are having a busy day here.

Mr. Park Yes we are. How may I help you Sir?

Mr. Jones I would like to buy a ticket.

Mr. Park Certainly sir. May I have your name please?

Mr. Jones Yes, Albert Jones.

Mr. Park The spelling is J-O-N-E-S initial A. Is that correct Mr. Jones?

Mr. Jones That's it.

Mr. Park And what are your destination and preferred dates of travel Mr. Jones?

Mr. Jones I want to go to Los Angeles on April 4, returning April 17.

Mr. Park Would you prefer First, Business or Economy Class, Mr. Jones?

Mr. Jones Business Class please.

Mr. Park Mr. Jones, I'll check that for you now.
Thank you for waiting. We have seats available on Smile Airlines flight 10 to Los Angeles on April 4 and flight 11 for your return trip on April 17. Will you be traveling by yourself or do you require additional seats Mr. Jones?

Mr. Jones I'll be going with my wife.

Mr. Park May I have her initial please?

Mr. Jones Yes, M.

Mr. Park So that's Mrs. M. Jones. May I have your passport please?

Mr. Jones Yes. Here it is.

Mr. Park Thank you. Mr. Jones, would you like to make a seat selection for you now?

Mr. Jones Yes, please. We'd like two seats in the window section. A window and aisle. I definitely do not want a middle seat.

Mr. Park Certainly, Mr. Jones. I'll check that for you now.
Thank you for waiting. I have reserved window and aisle seats 15A and B for you and Mrs. Jones.

	Would you like the same seats for your return flight on April 17?
Mr. Jones	Yes, that would be fine.
Mr. Park	May I have a contact number for you in Seoul?
Mr. Jones	Yes, my office number is 2645-0941.
Mr. Park	Thank you. Are you and Mrs. Jones smile airlines mileage members?
Mr. Jones	Yes, here are our smile airlines mileage cards.
Mr. Park	Fine. I'll put those in the computer right away. Your mileage will be tracked automatically. As I mentioned you are booked in Business Class, round trip to Los Angeles. The fare is 4,550,000 won. How would you like to pay for the ticket Mr. Jones?
Mr. Jones	By credit card. Do you take Visa?
Mr. Park	Certainly Mr. Jones. Would you please wait a moment while I process your card? Thank you for waiting. May I have your signature here please?
Mr. Jones	Oh sure.
Mr. Park	Thank you. Mr. Jones, here is your credit card and receipt. Here is your passport. This is your ticket and a copy of your itinerary. Let me recap it for you. You and Mrs. Jones are booked on smile airlines

10 from Seoul to Los Angeles on April 4 departing at 5:30 PM. You are booked on smile airlines 11 from Los Angeles back to Seoul on April 17 departing at 9:30AM. I have reserved you Business class seats in the window section, window seat 15A and aisle seat 15B.

Mr. Jones That sounds fine.

Mr. Park For your information the airport tax is 25,000 won. To make your trip more relaxing, may I suggest that you check in at least one and a half hours before departure time?

Mr. Jones Yes sure.

Mr. Park Is there anything else I can help you with today Mr. Jones?

Mr. Jones No everything is clear, thanks.

Mr. Park Thank you for choosing Smile Airlines Mr. Jones. I hope you and Mrs. Jones have a pleasant trip to Los Angeles.

Mr. Jones Thanks. Good bye.

Mr. Park Good bye Mr. Jones.

Situation 3 Selling smile airlines mileage program

• ***words and phrases***

smile airlines mileage program	Enroll
Automatically accumulate	Temporary card
Benefits	Sign your name here
Free ticket	smile airlines mileage program
benefits	
Mileage program service center	

Ms. Kim: *smile airlines Ticketing staff* | **Mrs. Troy**: Customer

Mrs. Troy has come into the Ticketing office to buy a ticket. During the transaction, Ms. Kim asks Mrs. Troy if she is a smile airlines mileage program member.

Ms. Kim Are you a smile airlines mileage program member Mrs. Troy?

Mrs. Troy I have heard of it but I have never bothered to join. What is it exactly?

Ms. Kim smile airlines mileage program is a mileage credit program which provides a lot of benefits if you travel frequently.

Mrs. Troy I never traveled much in the past but now that I live in Korea, I'll be back to the States twice a year.

Ms. Kim May I enroll you in our mileage program Mrs. Troy? Each time you fly with smile airlines, you automatically accumulate credits, which add up quite quickly. For example, when you accumulate only 20,000 points, you are eligible for a free economy class ticket anywhere in the United States. As you are traveling to Philadelphia, you can earn 17,000 points towards a free ticket.

Mrs. Troy That sounds quite good. How much does it cost?

Ms. Kim It is free to join. If you like, I can arrange for you to get credits for all of your future travel with smile airlines, starting with this flight.

Mrs. Troy OK, why not!

Ms. Kim If you fill in the form now I can give you a temporary card. May I help you fill out the smile airlines mileage program form?

Mrs. Troy Oh that's OK. I just fill in my name and address, right?

Ms. Kim Yes that's right, and sign your name here please. Thank you. Mrs. Troy, here is your temporary card. The number is very important as all your smile airlines Mileage will be credited to this account in the future. Please always give this number to the travel agent or the smile airlines staff when making your bookings.

Mrs. Troy I understand.

Ms. Kim You can also double check at the airport when you check-in to make sure the number is correct. Please have all of your tickets issued in the exact name you have just used to enroll. The name and number need to match exactly to enable you to receive your mileage credit.

Mrs. Troy Ok, I will do that.

Ms. Kim Thank you for choosing Smile Airlines, Mrs. Troy. I am sure you will enjoy your smile airlines mileage program benefits. If you do have any further questions on the program, our smile airlines mileage program service center will be happy to help you. This is their number.

Mrs. Troy Great, thanks for bringing this to my attention.

Ms. Kim You are welcome.

브뤼셀 항공brussels airlines

브뤼셀 항공은 2001년 파산한 벨기에의 사베나sabena 벨기에 항공을 대신하기 위해 2006년 설립된 벨기에의 항공사이다. 벨기에 브뤼셀에 본사가 있지만, 아프리카 노선이 강점인 만큼 광고도 아프리카가 생각나는 표범, 기린무늬 등을 활용하여 고객들에게 어필하고 있다.

Situation 4 Transfer a call to the Smile airlines mileage program center

• *words and phrases*

Immediate answer	Transfer
Calculate	Please hold the line, Mr. Strong
The line is engaged	

Ms. Park: *smile airlines Ticketing staff* | **Mr. Strong**: Customer

Ms. Park Good afternoon, smile airlines ticketing office. This is Ms. Park speaking.
How may I help you?

Mr. Strong Hi. I want to know how many smile airlines miles I have accumulated.

Ms. Park Certainly Sir. Our smile airlines mileage program staff will be happy to assist you. May I have your name please?

Mr. Strong Yes, Ed Strong.

Ms. Park Mr. Strong, may I transfer your call to the smile airlines mileage program center?
They will be able to calculate your mileage and give you an immediate answer.

Mr. Strong Sure. That's fine.

Ms. Park Please hold the line Mr. Strong.

Thank you for waiting. I am afraid the line is engaged Mr. Strong. May I have your telephone number and I will have one of our staff from the smile airlines mileage program center call you back?

Mr. Strong Sure. It's 290-0405. I'll be here until 5:00PM.

Ms. Park Thank you Mr. Strong. One of our staff will certainly call you back before 5:00PM. And thank you for calling smile airlines.

Mr. Strong Good bye.

Ms. Park Good bye Mr. Strong.

Situation 5 Fares

• *words and phrases*

Fare enquiry	Fixed
Information	Economy fares
Endorsed to	Handling fee
Normal fare	Refundable
Special economy fare	Open return
Stopovers	Flexibility
Competitive	

Ms. Lee: smile airlines Ticketing staff | **Ms. Broad**: Customer

After Ms. Lee has greeted Ms. Broad in the Ticketing office, Ms. Broad asks about fares to Boston.

Ms. Broad I'd like some information on Economy fares to Boston please?

Ms. Lee Certainly Ms. Broad. We offer two different fares, normal fare and special economy fare.

Ms. Broad Can you explain the difference?

Ms. Lee I would be happy to. With the normal fare, the travel dates can be fixed or open. The ticket can be endorsed to other carriers and is fully refundable. The price for the normal economy fare to Boston is 1,550,000 Won.

Ms. Broad So I can have open dates and change to other airlines with no extra charge if I want. Is that right?

Ms. Lee Yes right. The special fare varies according to the season. It has a fixed departure date and open return. On this type of fare, you are allowed two free stopovers in each direction. It is also endorsable and can be refunded but there would be a handling fee to do this. The cost of the special fare is 1,120,000 Won.

Ms. Broad I wonder which would be better for me.

Ms. Lee For customers who need flexibility, we recommend the normal fare. Otherwise, you will find our special fares very competitive.

Ms. Broad Well, my dates are pretty firm. I think the special fare would be fine.

Ms. Lee Certainly Ms. Broad. Would you like me to make a booking for you now?

Ms. Broad Yes. That would be fine.

Ms. Kim finishes the transaction in the normal way.

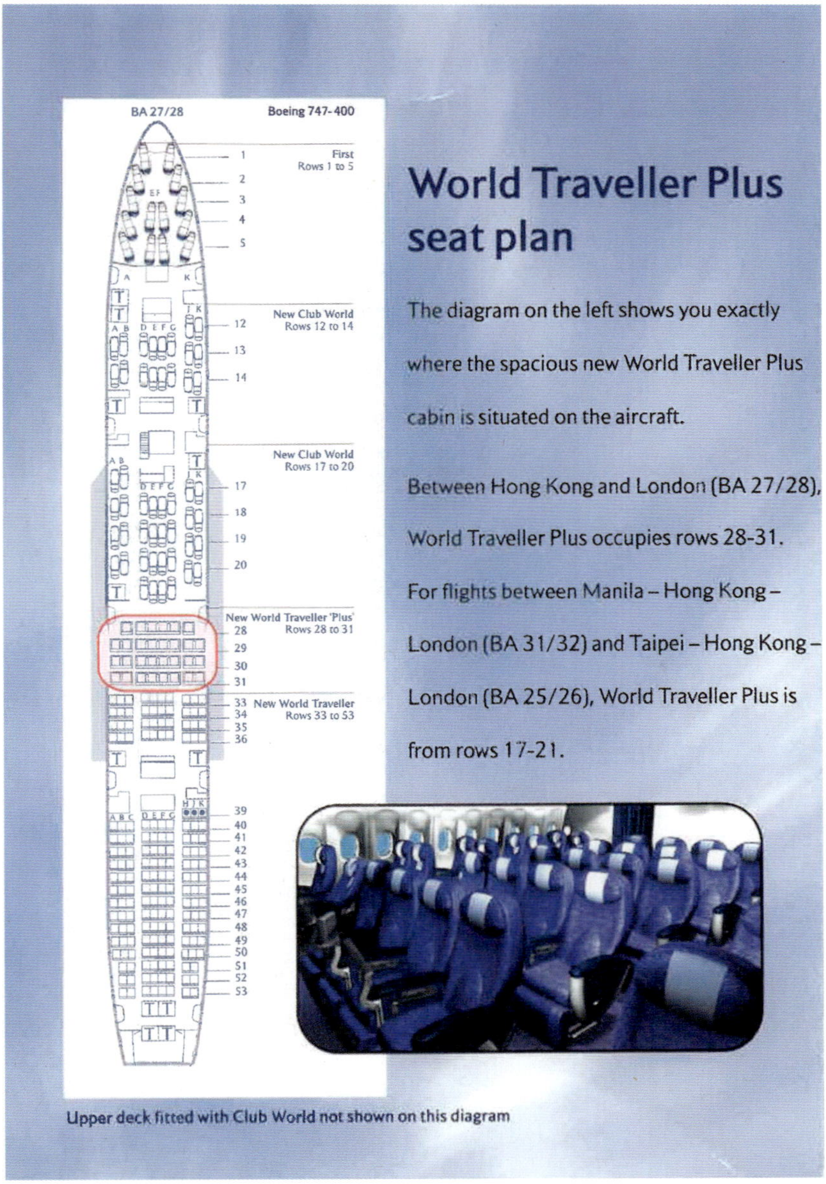

영국항공british airways

제1차 세계대전 종전 직후인 1919년 8월 25일 세계 최초로 런던과 파리를 연결하는 정기선 취항을 개시한 영국항공은 런던의 히드로 공항과 게이트 윅 공항을 중심으로 유럽, 아프리카, 미주 등 전 세계 105개국 260여 주요 도시를 운항하고 있다.

Situation 6 Change booking

• *words and phrases*

Original booking	I do understand your concern
Availability	Reissue
Special round trip ticket	Once again let me apologize
Additional charge	Misunderstanding
Weekend travel	

Mr. Yoo: smile airlines Ticketing staff | **Mr. Brown**: Customer

Mr. Yoo has greeted Mr. Brown in the Ticketing office. Mr. Brown has come in to change his travel dates.

Mr. Brown I would like to change my departure date to May 11 instead of the 9th.

Mr. Yoo Certainly Sir. May I have your ticket please?

Mr. Brown Here you are.

Mr. Yoo Mr. Brown, your original booking was Thursday, May 9 Seoul to New York on smile airlines flight 18. Is that right?

Mr. Brown Right.

Mr. Yoo I'll just check the availability of the flight on May 11 for you.

Thank you for waiting. Mr. Brown, the ticket you are holding is a special round trip ticket which is good for travel Monday through Thursday. I can extend it to cover Saturday travel but there would be an additional charge of USD 55. Would you like me to do that?

Mr. Brown My travel agent in the States said I could change the dates of my departure. He never said anything about a charge for weekend travel! Why is there an extra charge?

Mr. Yoo Let me explain. The ticket you have is offered at a special fare. This code here means that you may change your travel dates but if you choose to fly on a Friday, Saturday or Sunday, there is an additional charge of USD 55. If you prefer Mr. Brown, I can change your booking for a weekday.

Mr. Brown I just wish I had been told about this before.

Mr. Yoo I do understand your concern Mr. Brown and I am sorry there has been a misunderstanding about your ticket. Will you be able to travel on your original Thursday booking or if you prefer, we have seats available on the following Monday, May 13?

Mr. Brown I guess you had better book me for Monday May 13.

Mr. Yoo Certainly Mr. Brown, I'll reserve that for you now. Would you mind waiting about five minutes while I reissue your ticket?

Mr. Yoo finished the transaction as usual and bids farewell.

Mr. Yoo Mr. Brown, I hope you enjoy your flight to New York. Once again let me apologize that there was a misunderstanding with your ticket.

Mr. Brown Never mind. I think we have things sorted out now. Good bye.

Mr. Yoo Good bye Mr. Brown.

유나이티드항공united airlines

1930년 세계 최초로 승무원 제도를 도입한 유나이티드항공의 Easy Check-in은 수하물checked baggage이 없는 승객들이 카운터 직원의 도움 없이 직접 체크인을 할 수 있는 새로운 서비스이다.

Situation 7 Lost ticket

• words and phrases

Ticket	Lost
Last name	Misplaced
Initial	I am very sorry to hear that
Flight details	May I ask you
Credit card receipt	A record of your ticket purchase
Lost ticket form	

Ms. Kim: smile airlines Ticketing staff | **Mr. Colin**: Customer

As Ms. Kim greets Mr. Colin she can see he is very upset. He tells her he has lost his ticket.

Mr. Colin I am very worried. I seem to have misplaced my ticket. I really don't know what to do!

Ms. Kim I am very sorry to hear that, sir. Don't worry. Let me see what I can do to help. May I have your last name please?

Mr. Colin Yes, Colin.

Ms. Kim May I ask you to spell that for me?

Mr. Colin C-O-L-I-N.

Ms. Kim C-O-L-I-N. And the initial of your first name please?

Mr. Colin Yes, W.

Ms. Kim Thank you Mr. Colin. May I have your flight details please.

Mr. Colin Yes, I am supposed to fly to Tokyo on November 12, Business Class.

Ms. Kim I'll just check your booking now. Ah, here it is. Mr. Colin, do you have a record of your ticket purchase such as a credit card receipt or a receipt from your travel agent?

Mr. Colin I do have the credit card slip. I'm glad I've got that. Here it is.

Ms. Kim Thank you. I will fill in the lost ticket form for you.

(Ms. Kim politely asks for details needed.)

Thank you Mr. Colin. May I have your passport please?

Mr. Colin, I will reissue your ticket now. There will be an additional charge of USD 150.

Mr. Colin OK, fine.

Ms. Kim processes the credit card, recaps the itinerary and closes the visit as usual.

Situation 8 Ticket endorsement

• *words and phrases*

Departure times	Endorsed
Options	May I ask why?
Extra space	Convenient
Complimentary dinner	I prefer
Overseas phone call	Block
Arrival details	

Mr. Park: *smile airlines Ticketing staff* | **Mrs. Stone**: Customer

Mr. Park Good afternoon. My name is Mr. Park. How may I help you?

Mrs. Stone I'd like to cancel my booking on smile airlines and have my ticket endorsed.

Mr. Park May I have your ticket please? Thank you. Which airline would you like your ticket endorsed to, Mrs. Stone?

Mrs. Stone Jupiter Airlines.

Mr. Park May I ask why you would like to change to Jupiter Airlines?

Mrs. Stone Their departure times are more convenient for me and I prefer their service.

Mr. Park Oh I see. Mrs. Stone, we sure would hate to lose your business. Let me give you a few options to consider if you decide to stay with us on smile airlines.

Mrs. Stone What do you mean?

Mr. Park Well, I can block the seat next to you on our flight so that you have some extra space. Also, since Jupiter Airlines does depart a little earlier than we do, I would be happy to offer you and one guest a complimentary dinner at any of the airport restaurants.

Mrs. Stone Gee, that sounds alright. I do like to have a bit of extra space.

Mr. Park I would also be happy to pay for an overseas phone call or send any faxes free of charge to let your company know your arrival details.

Mrs. Stone Gosh, smile airlines really wants my business.

Mr. Park We certainly do value your business Mrs. Stone. May I reconfirm the smile airlines flight for you now?

Mrs. Stone Yes, I have changed my mind.

Mr. Park reconfirms the flight, blocks the next seat, recaps the flight details and closes by thanking Mrs. Stone again for flying smile airlines.

Mr. Park Mrs. Stone, let me thank you again for flying smile airlines. I hope you enjoy our service to Tokyo.

Mrs. Stone Thank you Mr. Park. You have been very helpful. Good bye.

Mr. Park Good bye Mrs. Stone.

항공상식 3 항공기용 피뢰침, 정전기 방출기

만에 하나 벼락을 맞게 되면 비행기에는 어떤 일이 생길까?

이러한 질문에 항공전문가들과 엔지니어들은 한결같이 벼락을 맞더라도 기체와 그 운항에 있어서 안전은 99.9% 보장할 수 있다고 말한다. 모든 비행기에는 번개로부터 승객의 안전을 지킬 수 있는 번개 보호장치가 마련돼 있기 때문이다.

우선 모든 여객기에는 웨더 레이더라는 특수 전파탐지기가 탑재돼 있어 문제성 구름을 조기에 발견할 수 있다는 것. 이 레이더는 구름의 두께와 그 구름이 지닌 전기량까지 측정해 알려주기 때문에 기장이 미리 위험을 피해 우회 비행할 수 있도록 경고해 준다. 설사 벼락이 치는 기상조건에 부딪힌다 해도 안전에는 별 문제가 없다. 항공기에는 좌우 날개 및 꼬리날개 등에 일종의 항공기용 피뢰침인 정전기 방출기가 달려 있기 때문이다.

항공기가 번개에 맞을 경우에 전기는 20~30cm 길이의 이 뾰족한 부분을 통해 순식간에 공기 중으로 방전된다. 또 전기가 순간적으로 동체를 따라 흐르게 하려면 항공기 전체를 하나의 전선처럼 연결해 줘야 한다. 그래야 전기가 한 곳에 뭉쳐 있지 않고 분산되면서 쉽게 뾰족한 침을 통해 날아가 버릴 수 있다. 이 때문에 항공기 표면은 대개 가로, 세로 1m 이상 되는 대형 알루미늄 판들을 이어 만드는데 이 조각을 이은 부분(리벳)을 따라 전기가 흐르도록 설계돼 있어 항공기 동체 전체가 하나의 커다란 전기회로를 형성하고 있다. 전기회로가 끊어진 부분은 본딩 와이어라는 특수 전선을 사용해 연결하며 이 전기의 길은 연료탱크 같이 폭발의 우려가 있는 곳은 피하고 계기판 등 전기에 민감한 각종 전기장치에도 영향을 미치지 않도록 설치돼 있다. 무엇보다 객실 쪽과는 철저히 단절돼 있어 승객들이 전기쇼크 등에 노출되지 않도록 하는 것이 회로 설계의 최대 노하우라고 할 수 있다.

영국항공british airways

항공사 동맹체 원월드의 창립항공사이다. 허브 공항은 런던 히드로 국제공항과 런던 개트윅 국제공항이다. 영국항공은 런던에서 싱가포르까지의 목적지 노선 광고를 흥미로운 사진과 함께 고객에게 보여주며 긴 비행시간이지만 편안한 비행을 강조하고 있다.

Section 4

AIRPORT PASSENGER SERVICE

Objectives

To extend your English vocabulary in Airline Service industry.

To role-play various airport situations with a focus on appropriate service English.

To practice using polite and positive assertive English to deal with very demanding passenger situations.

To discuss real life situations observed at the airport and develop strategies in English to delight customers.

Unit 1

Check-in counter

Situation 1 Check in(economy class)

• ***words and phrases***

Sir / Madam	Ticket
May I	Passport
Smile Airlines Flight	Final destination
Bags	Suitcase
Baggage	Scale
Check-in	Name tags
Confirm	Bound for
Baggage claim stub	Reserved seat
United States Customs	Concierge
I see that	I would like to confirm
Would you prefer	Would that be alright?
How may I help you?	Please wait a moment
Thank you for waiting	

Ms. Kim: smile airlines Check-in staff | **Mr. Butler**: Passenger

Ms. Kim	Good morning and thank you for waiting.
Mr. Butler	Good morning.
Ms. Kim	May I have your ticket and passport please?
Mr. Butler	Yes, sure.
Ms. Kim	Thank you. Are you traveling by yourself today, Mr. Butler?
Mr. Butler	Yes, I am.
Ms. Kim	Please wait a moment while I check your booking. I see that you are traveling on Smile Airlines flight 24 to Los Angeles today. Is that your final destination?
Mr. Butler	Yes it is.
Ms. Kim	How many bags would you like to check-in?
Mr. Butler	I have two suitcases.
Ms. Kim	Please place your bags on the scale.
Mr. Butler	Alright.
Ms. Kim	Thank you. Mr. Butler, I see you have no name tags on your luggage. Would you kindly write your name, address and phone number on these tags? I'll attach them to your bags for you.
Mr. Butler	Yes, of course. That's a good idea.
Ms. Kim	Thank you very much. Mr. Butler, I would like to confirm that I am checking-in two pieces of bagg-

age on Smile Airlines flight 24, bound for Los Angeles Is that correct?

Mr. Butler Yes, that's right.

Ms. Kim I will put your baggage claim stubs onto your ticket for you. Mr. Butler, would you like a window or an aisle seat?

Mr. Butler I prefer a window seat.

Ms. Kim Certainly Mr. Butler, I have window seat 47A for you. Would that be alright?

Mr. Butler Yes that is fine.

Ms. Kim Mr. Butler, here is your return ticket and passport. These are your claim stubs for your two pieces of baggage checked through to Los Angeles.

This is your boarding pass. Your flight number is Smile Airlines flight 24 to Los Angeles.

You have window seat 47A.

We will begin boarding at 10:15 through gate number 5.

The gate is located beyond the Passport control area. As this gate becomes quite busy, may I suggest that you go to the gate no later than 9:15.

Mr. Butler Yes, I understand.

Ms. Kim Mr. Butler, thank you for choosing Smile Airlines. Please enjoy your flight.

제주항공jeju air

대한민국의 저비용 항공사인 제주항공의 광고이다.
수하물이 없는데 왜 수하물 비용을 낼까?, 왜 기내식은 두 가지 종류에서 선택해야 할까? 등 승객의 입장에서 저비용항공사의 강점을 어필하고 있다.

Situation 2 Check in(business or first)

Ms. Wun: smile airlines check in staff | **Mrs. Jones**: Passenger

Ms. Wun	Good afternoon, may I help you, ma'am?
Mrs. Jones	Yes, thank you.
Ms. Wun	May I have your ticket and passport please?
Mrs. Jones	Here they are.
Ms. Wun	Thank you. Mrs. Jones, I see that there are two traveling today. Is that correct?
Mrs. Jones	Yes, my husband and myself.
Ms. Wun	Certainly Mrs. Jones. Please wait a moment while I check your booking. Thank you for waiting. How many bags would you like to check-in today, Mrs. Jones?
Mrs. Jones	We have three suitcases.
Ms. Wun	Certainly, our concierge will help you put your baggage on the scale. Mrs. Jones, as you and Mr. Jones are traveling with us in First Class, I'm placing doorside tags on your baggage. This means your bags will be off loaded first in Los Angeles.

Mrs. Jones	Oh, that's good.
Ms. Wun	I would like to confirm with you that I will be checking 3 suitcases on Smile Airlines flight 24 bound for your final destination to Los Angeles. Is that correct?
Mrs. Jones	Yes, that's right.
Ms. Wun	Fine, I will put your baggage claim stubs onto your ticket. Mrs. Jones, we have reserved seat 2E and 2F on the right side of our First class cabin for you today as you requested.
Mrs. Jones	Mm'mm.
Ms. Wun	Here are your onward tickets and passports, Mrs. Jones, and these are your baggage claim checks for your three suitcases checked to Los Angeles. You will be clearing United States customs at Los Angeles. These are your boarding passes. You will notice that we begin boarding through gate number 5 at 2:30. Mrs. Jones, may I invite you and Mr. Jones to our World Club Lounge, located at the departure hall? You can relax there until our flight is ready for boarding.
Mrs. Jones	That sounds nice. Where did you say it is located?

Ms. Wun	Mrs. Jones, our concierge will escort you to the lounge if you wish.
Ms. Jones	Oh, great. I'm terrible with directions.
Ms. Wun	Mrs. Jones, thank you for choosing Smile Airlines. I do hope you enjoy your flight.

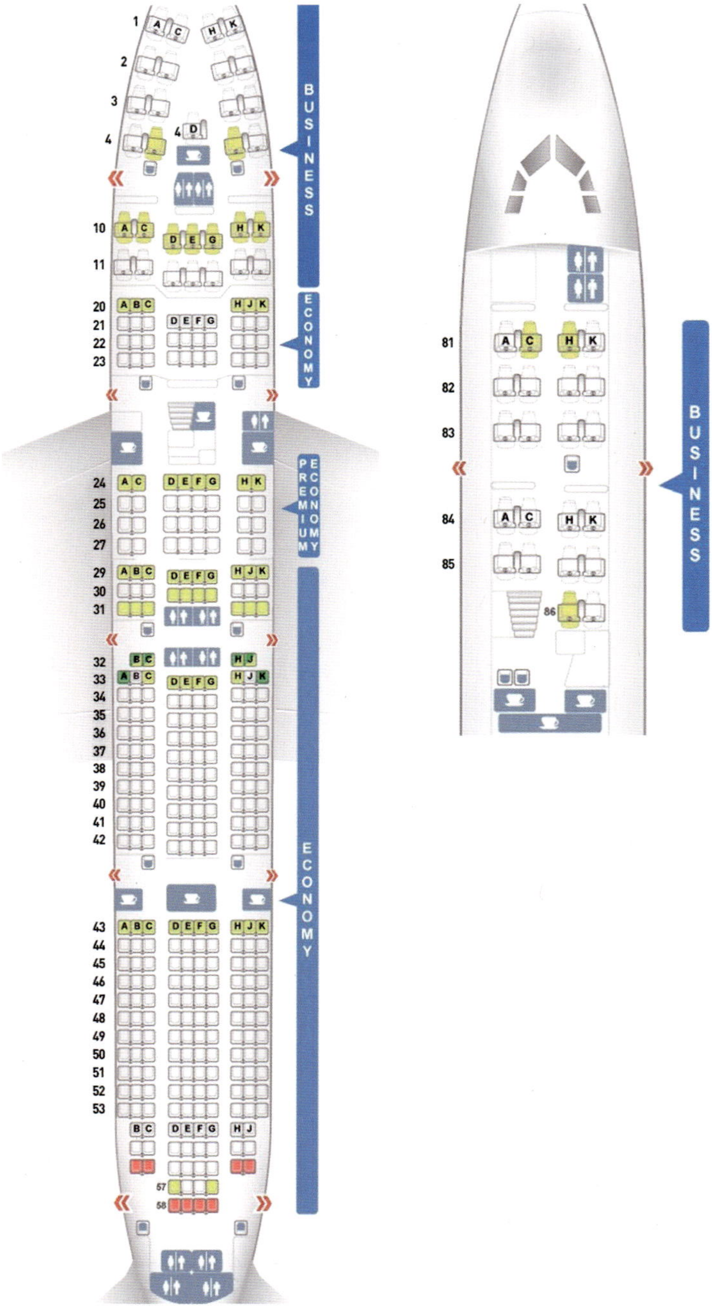

보잉747-400기종의 일반적인 좌석 배치

Situation 3 Wheelchair passenger

• ***words and phrases***

Wheelchair	It is my pleasure
Security	Please have a seat
Immigration	Would you follow me please?
We can arrange	

Mr. Allan: 80year-old passenger | **Mrs. Martin**: Mr. Allan's daughter
Mr. Lee: smile airlines Check-in staff | **Mr. Kil**: smile airlines staff

Mr. Lee Good afternoon. May I help you?

Mrs. Martin Oh yes, thank you. We are checking in to Chicago.

Mr. Lee Certainly Ma'am. May I have your ticket and passports please?

Mrs. Martin Here they are.

Mr. Lee Mrs. Martin, I see there are two of you checking in today on Smile Airlines flight 20 to Seattle with a connection to Chicago.

Mrs. Martin Yes that is right, I'm traveling with my father.

Mr. Lee Certainly Mrs. Martin. Would Mr. Allan like any assistance through immigration and onto the aircraft?

Mrs. Martin What kind of assistance do you offer?

Mr. Lee Well, Mrs. Martin as it is quite a distance to the aircraft, we can arrange a wheelchair for Mr. Allan. One of our staff will escort you both through immigration and security and then take you to the aircraft.

Mrs. Martin Oh, that would be quite helpful. My father has no difficulty walking but he does get tired over long distances.

Mr. Lee I understand. I will make the arrangements for you, Mrs. Martin. Just let me finish checking you in.

After finishing the check-in process

Mr. Lee Mrs. Martin, our staff, Mr. Kil will meet you at our information counter just over there at 3:15. He will be wearing a uniform like mine. Mr. Kil will take you and Mr. Allan right onto your flight. In the meantime, there is a coffee shop over there where you can relax until 3:15 if you wish.

Mrs. Martin Many thanks.

Mr. Lee Certainly Mrs. Martin. It is my pleasure. I hope you both enjoy your flight.

3:15 at Information counter

Mr. Kil Excuse me, would you be Mrs. Martin and Mr. Allan?

Mr. Allan Yes, that's right.

Mr. Kil Good afternoon, my name is Mr. Kil from Smile Airlines. I will be escorting you onto our flight today.
I have a wheelchair ready for you right here.
Mr. Allan, please have a seat.

Mr. Allen Thank you.

Mr. Kil May I have your passports and boarding passes please?

Mr. Allen Yes, here they are.

Mr. Kil Great, we are ready to proceed through security and immigration. Mrs. Martin, would you follow me please?

Proceed through security and onto the aircraft. At the aircraft door or after the passenger is seated on the aircraft.

Mr. Kil Mrs. Martin, Mr. Allan, is there anything else I can do for you today?

Mrs. Martin No thank you. You have been most helpful.

Mr. Kil It was my pleasure. Thank you for choosing Smile Airlines. Have a pleasant flight.

싱가포르항공singapore airlines

1947년 5월 설립된 싱가포르항공은 조그만 지역항공사에서 세계 항공업계의 선두주자로 빠르게 성장하였다. 비즈니스 트래블러Business Traveller, 타임지 아시아Times Asia 등의 권위 있는 언론사에서 매년 최고의 항공사로 선정될 만큼 안전도, 기내서비스 등에서 세계적인 명성을 얻고 있다.

Situation 4 Seat is not available

• *words and phrases*

Our requested seat is not available	May I offer you
It is possible	At the last moment
In addition	You are welcome

Ms. Park: smile airlines Check-in staff | **Ms. Miller**: Passenger

Ms. Park	Ms. Miller would you like a window or an aisle seat?
Ms. Miller	A window seat please.
Ms. Park	I am sorry a window seat is not available. Instead, may I offer you an aisle seat, Ms. Miller?
Ms. Miller	An asile seat will be fine.
Ms. Park	Ms. Miller. I'll give you seat 19C. It is possible a window seat will become available at the last moment. May I ask you to check with our staff at the gate? They may be able to arrange a window seat for you.
Ms. Miller	Oh, alright.
Ms. Park	In addition, I will reserve you a window seat, number 19A on your return flight. Would that be alright?
Ms. Miller	Oh that's great. Thank you.
Ms. Park	You are welcome.

Situation 5 Reserved seats not available

• *words and phrases*

Hand baggage	Priority doorside tags
Baggage claim area	Supervisor
Return trip	Check your baggage through to
Unavailable	I am sorry there has been a problem with
Apologize	I do apologize
Would that be alright?	

Mr. Park: smile airlines Check-in staff | **Mrs. Jones**: Passenger

Mr. Park May I help you Ma'am?

Mrs. Jones Yes, thank you.

Mr. Park Good afternoon, Ma'am.
May I have your tickets and passports please?
Thank you.
Mrs. Jones, I see that there are three of you traveling with us in executive class today. Is that correct?

Mrs. Jones Yes, my mother, my son and myself.

Mr. Park Fine, and you are traveling on Smile Airlines flight number 20 to Seattle today. Is that your final destination?

Mrs. Jones No we are going to Salt Lake City.

Mr. Park Oh, I see. May I have your onward ticket please?

Mrs. Jones Yes here they are. I think we are connecting to United Airlines flight.

Mr. Park Certainly. I will check your luggage through to Salt Lake City. However you must pick up your bags in Seattle and clear United States customs there. After you have cleared customs you can give your bags to the United Airlines staff at the connecting desk. Your bags will go right through to Salt Lake city for you.

Mrs. Jones Can't you just send the bags right through?

Mr. Park I'm afraid not Mrs. Jones. You are required to clear customs at your first port of entry into the United States.

Mrs. Jones Oh, I see.

Mr. Park How many bags would you like to check-in?

Mrs. Jones We have six suitcases.

Mr. Park Certainly, please place your baggage on the scale.

Mrs. Jones Hand baggage too?

Mr. Park No, Mrs. Jones, just your check-in baggage. Thank you.

As you are traveling with us in Executive Class today, I am placing priority doorside tags on your luggage. Your suitcases will be unloaded first and sent to the baggage claim area in Seattle.

Mrs. Jones Oh, very good.

Mr. Park Mrs. Jones let me confirm that I will be checking in 6 pieces of baggage on Smile Airlines flight 20 to Seattle and connecting to United Airlines flight 14 bound for Salt Lake City. Is that correct?

Mrs. Jones Yes, and we clear customs in Seattle?

Mr. Park Yes, that is correct.

I will put your baggage claim stubs on your ticket.

Mrs. Jones Oh great.

Mr. Park Mrs. Jones, would you like seats in the front section of the cabin?

Mrs. Jones I reserved three seats in the front section, numbers 17 C, D and E.

Mr. Park I'm sorry Mrs. Jones, there has been a problem with your seat reservation. Unfortunately, 17 C, D, E are unavailable.

Mrs. Jones What do you mean? I booked those seats months ago!

Mr. Park Mrs. Jones, I do apologize for this problem with your seats.

What I can offer is the same three seats in row 21. Would that be alright?

Mrs. Jones Well I suppose so. But I think you should do something about your computer system. This happens quite often.

Mr. Park I will certainly make a note about this for my supervisor.

Thank you for bringing this to my attention.

In addition, let me reserve your requested seats for your return flight in order to avoid this problem again. You prefer seats 17 C, D, E. Is that correct?

Mrs. Jones Yes, Thank you.

Mr. Park Mrs. Jones here are your onward tickets and passport for you, your mother and son.

These are your baggage claim stubs for 6 pieces checked through to Salt Lake City.

Here are your boarding passes. Your flight is smile airlines flight number 20 to Seattle. You can get your onward boarding passes from the United Airlines staff in Seattle. Your seat numbers on our flight today are 21 C, D, E.

We will begin boarding at 2:30PM through gate number 2. At this time, I would like to invite you to our World Club Lounge. Here is an invitation card with a map on the back.

Mrs. Jones Oh, no thank you. We plan to do some shopping.

Mr. Park Certainly Mrs. Jones.

The gates are located right beyond the Passport Control area. As this area gets very busy, may I suggest you go to the gate no later than one hour before departure?

Mrs. Jones Thank you.

Mr. Park Thank you for choosing Smile Airlines Mrs. Jones.
We are happy to have the 3 of you aboard.

Situation 6 Excess baggage

• ***words and phrases***

Excess baggage	Excess charge
Waive	Weight change
Major credit card	Co-operation
Receipt for excess charges	Under the circumstances
Thank you for your cooperation	I will now prepare

Ms. Lee: smile airlines Check-in staff | **Mr. Black**: Passenger

Ms. Lee Good evening. Thank you for waiting.

Mr. Black Good evening.

Ms. Lee May I have your passport and ticket please?

Mr. Black Here they are.

Ms. Lee How many people in your party, Mr. Black?

Mr. Black Two of us, myself and my wife.

Ms. Lee Certainly, Mr. Black, I see that you are traveling on Smile Airlines flight 20 to Detroit today. Is that your final destination?

Mr. Black Yes, it is.

Ms. Lee Fine, how many bags would you like to check-in?

Mr. Black We have 6 pieces.

Ms. Lee Please place your bags on the scale.

Mr. Black Okay.

Ms. Lee Thank you. Mr. Black, you have 2 pieces of excess baggage.

The excess charge will be 240,000 won.

Mr. Black What do you mean excess! We are moving back to the States so we may have a few extra things. I usually travel well under the limit. Can't you make an exception for us today?

Ms. Lee I do understand your situation. Under the circumstances, I will waive the weight charge and only charge you for your two pieces of excess. In that case, the charge would be 200,000 won. Would that be alright Mr. Black?

Mr. Black Listen, I don't have that much cash and I really don't want to be bothered going to the bank.

Ms. Lee Mr. Black, I can put that on any major credit card if you prefer. How would that be?

Mr. Black Well, I suppose I have no choice!

Ms. Lee Thank you for your cooperation, Mr. Black.

I will now prepare the necessary forms for you. May I ask you to wait a moment?

Thank you for waiting Mr. Black.

May I ask you to take this form over to our information counter? You can pay the excess charge there and our staff will give you a receipt. I can then finish checking you in.

Mr. Black This is a bloody nuisance.

Mr. Black pays the excess charge and comes back to the counter.

Ms. Lee Mr. Black, I am sorry for this inconvenience. Do you and your wife prefer window or aisle seats?

Mr. Black We want window seats, ones with extra leg room if possible.

Ms. Lee Certainly Mr. Black. I can offer you seats 40 D and E. These seats are located in the bulkhead area. Would that be alright?

Mr. Black Yes, fine.

Ms. Lee Let me confirm, I have booked you in seats 40 D and E on Smile Airlines flight 20 to Detroit. I have checked six pieces of baggage to that destination. Here are your passports. I have attached your baggage stubs and your receipt for excess charges to your ticket here. This is your boarding pass.
The flight will begin boarding at 8:00PM through gate 1. The gate is located right beyond the passport control area. As this area becomes very busy, may I ask you to go the gate no later than one hour before departure?

Mr. Black Alright.

Ms. Lee Mr. Black, I hope you and your wife enjoy your trip.

에어프랑스air france

이 광고는 멕시코에서 패션의 도시 파리로의 목적지 광고이지만 글로벌 환경 문제를 생각하는 친환경 항공사로서의 이미지를 고객들에게 어필하고 있다.

Situation 7 Released booking

• ***words and phrases***

Confirmed booking
Priority waitlist
I do understand
Were you able
We did not receive your reconfirmation
There are several options I can offer you
If you prefer
I will do that for you now
In the future may I ask you to
Problem will be avoided
I'm sorry for the inconvenience this has caused you.
I'm pleased to tell you
Please proceed directly to

Mr. Harris: *Executive class passenger* | **Mr. Moon**: *smile airlines staff*
Ms. Choi: *smile airlines first class staff*

Mr. Moon Good morning. May I help you?

Mr. Harris Yes, I'm checking-in for your LA flight.

Mr. Moon Certainly Sir. May I have your passport and ticket please?

Mr. Harris Here they are.

Mr. Moon I see there is just one person traveling today. Is that correct?

Mr. Harris Yes.

Mr. Moon Mr. Harris. Please wait one moment while I check your booking.

Thank you for waiting. Mr. Harris, may I ask you if you were able to reconfirm your booking?

Mr. Harris To tell you the truth, I have been out in the countryside and I was unable to make a call to reconfirm. Why, is there a problem?

Mr. Moon I'm sorry, Mr. Harris, but because we did not receive a reconfirmation, your reservation has been automatically released. Unfortunately our flight today is quite full.

Mr. Harris Oh, I can't believe it! I felt sure that an Executive Class seat would be alright. What am I going to do now? I have a very important meeting in the States.

Mr. Moon I'm sorry, Mr. Harris. I know this is very frustrating. I do understand you must be very upset.

However, there are several options I can offer you today, Mr. Harris.

Mr. Harris What are they?

Mr. Moon Well, I can put you on a priority waitlist for today's flight.

That way if a seat becomes available at the last minute, we can offer that to you.

Mr. Harris What are my chances of getting on?

Mr. Moon I am afraid we won't know until just before we close our check-in counter, about 45 minutes before departure. We would ask you to come back to our counter at 10:30 at which time we would know if a seat had become available.

Mr. Harris Are there any other options available?

Mr. Moon Certainly Mr. Harris. I can make a confirmed booking for you on tomorrow's flight or, if you prefer, we have a flight with seats available this afternoon to Seattle. I could re-route you to Los Angeles through Seattle. Which would you prefer?

Mr. Harris Well, I definitely can't wait until tomorrow.

Mr. Moon In that case, may I suggest I put you on our priority wait-list for today's direct flight to Los Angeles and make a confirmed booking for this afternoon's flight to Seattle with a smile airlines connection to Los Angeles.

Mr. Harris Well I guess under the circumstances I'd better do that.

Mr. Moon Certainly Mr. Harris, I'll do that for you now. May I ask you to come back to our First class counter by 10:30 and our staff there will inform you if seats are available? I will pass your ticket to our First class staff.

Is that alright?

Mr. Harris Yes, thank you for your help.

Mr. Moon Certainly Mr. Harris, it is my pleasure. I know how difficult it is to reconfirm from outside of the city. In the future, may I recommend you reconfirm your flight with us before you leave Seoul? In that way, this problem will be avoided in the future.

Mr. Harris Yes, I will certainly do that. So I should come back at 10:30?

Mr. Moon That is right Mr. Harris. I'm so sorry for the inconvenience this has caused you.

■ *At 10:30*

Ms. Choi Yes sir, how may I help you.

Mr. Harris I am waitlisted on your flight to Los Angeles today, my name is Harris.

Ms. Choi Certainly Mr. Harris, I will check that for you now. Thank you for waiting Mr. Harris. I am pleased to tell you we have a seat available for you on Smile Airlines flight 24 to Los Angeles.

Mr. Harris Oh, I'm so relieved.

Ms. Choi I'll just finish checking you in now.

After checking-in

Ms. Choi As it is so close to departure time Mr. Harris, may I ask you to proceed directly through the security area and to gate 3 for boarding?

Mr. Harris Yes, I'm on my way.

Ms. Choi I'm sorry for any inconvenience the situation has caused you. I hope you enjoy your flight.

Situation 8 Delayed flight

• words and phrases

Overnight accommodation
I am sorry inform you that
Our flight has been delayed
To the best of my knowledge
New estimated time of departure
Onward flight information
I do understand your concern
We are doing everything possible
We have prepared this delay package
If you have any questions
Our staff will make alternate arrangements
We expect a lengthy delay
We have arranged
Thank you for your understanding

Ms. Park: smile airlines staff | **Mr. Harper**: Passenger

▪ *Short Delay*

Ms. Park May I help you sir?

Mr. Harper Yes, thanks.

Ms. Park Good morning. May I have your ticket and passport please, sir?

Thank you, Mr. Harper. I see you are booked on Smile Airlines flight 29 to Taipei. Is that correct?

Mr. Harper Yes, that's right.

Ms. Park Mr. Harper, I am very sorry to inform you that your flight with us has been delayed due to bad weather. The new estimated time of departure will be 10:00AM.

Mr. Harper Yes, I heard about a typhoon on the radio. Are you sure the flight will only be delayed an hour?

Ms. Park To the best of my knowledge, the flight will depart at 10:50. If there is any further delay, our staff will be making up-dated announcements to keep you informed. I'm very sorry about the inconvenience.

Mr. Harper Oh well, it's not your fault.

Ms. Park Mr. Harper, let me finish checking you in right now. Are you traveling by yourself today?

Over 90 Minute Delay

Ms. Park Mr. Harper, I am very sorry your flight with us today has been delayed due to maintenance.
The new estimated time of departure will be 4:30 this afternoon.

Mr. Harper What! That's 5 hours from now!

Ms. Park I do understand your concern. We are doing everything possible to ensure to your safety and comfort. We have prepared this delay package which contains a meal voucher, fax paper, a message form and instructions on your entitlements. If you have any questions please ask one of our staff at the information counter.

Now Mr. Harper, I will finish checking you in.

■ *Estimated Departure Unknown*

Ms. Park I'am very sorry for the inconvenience but our flight today will be delayed because of the late incoming aircraft.

At this time, we are not certain about the precise length of delay or departure time.

Mr. Harper Well. What am I supposed to do now? Just wait around?

Ms. Park Mr. Harper, I will finish checking you in. Then may I ask you to proceed directly to departure gate 3?

Our staff will be making updated announcements every 30 minutes to keep you informed. If the delay is a lengthy one, our staff will make alternate arrangements for you if necessary.

Overnight Delay

Ms. Park Mr. Harper, I am very sorry to inform you that your flight today with us has been delayed due to bad weather.

We expect a lengthy delay so we have arranged overnight accommodation for you at the Royal hotel.

Mr. Harper You mean I have to stay overnight? That's ridiculous! I have an important meeting in the United States. Can't you book me on another flight?

Ms. Park I do understand your concern Mr. Harper. Unfortunately, there are no flights on any carrier to the US before tomorrow morning.

Mr. Harper This is outrageous!

Ms. Park Let me assure you we have made all the arrangements to make your stay in Seoul as comfortable as possible. Here is a Delay Package with your hotel and onward flight information as well as a fax form so we can advise your contacts in the States of your delay.

Once again, let me apologize for this delay. A smile airlines staff will accompany you to the hotel and can answer any of your questions.

We will of course keep you informed of the progress of the delay through the staff at your hotel. I am so sorry about this delayed flight.

Mr. Harper I will suppose under the circumstances, this is the best that can be done.

Ms. Park Thank you for understanding. See you tomorrow Mr. Harper.

항공상식 4

기내에서의 환기

1만 3천~5천m의 상공을 비행하는 여객기의 외부 온도는 무려 영하 50~60℃에 가깝다. 그리고 기압은 지상의 15 정도밖에 되질 않는다. 하지만 여객기의 객실 내에서는 외부 변화와 관계없이 지상에서와 똑같이 쾌적한 상태의 온도와 기압이 유지된다.

이러한 비행기의 에너지 원인은 엔진을 통해 쾌적한 공기를 만들어내는 것이다. 영하 50℃ 이하의 차가운 외부공기를 그대로 기내에 들어오게 할 수는 없기 때문에, 들어온 공기를 압축기에서 압축해 2백60℃ 정도의 아주 뜨거운 고온·고압의 공기를 만든 다음 이 뜨거운 공기의 일부를 분리해 열교환기와 공기순환장치에서 외부 공기를 이용, 냉각시킨 뒤 객실로 보내 항상 일정한 온도를 유지하는 것이다. 그러나 객실은 완전 밀폐된 공간이므로 환기가 문제된다. 사람이 호흡하면서 인체에 산소를 공급하듯이 여객기도 인체와 똑같이 호흡하면서 객실에 깨끗한 공기를 공급하고 있다. 사람은 1분에 약 6ℓ의 공기를 호흡한다. 따라서 4백명이 탑승하는 경우에는 2천4백ℓ의 공기가 필요하다.

참고로 여객기는 1분에 20ℓ짜리 1천2백 드럼 분량의 신선한 공기를 제공할 수 있는 기능이 있다. 이것은 여객기가 4백명 만석일 때 한 사람당 1분 동안에 3드럼의 공기를 마실 수 있는 양이므로 실제 승객이 흡수하는 양의 거의 10배에 가깝다. 결국 객실의 공기는 거의 3~4분에 한 번씩 신선한 공기로 환기되고 있다.

Unit 2

Concierge and lounge

• *words and phrases*

May I invite you to
Lounge representative
Please follow me
If there is anything else I can do for you please do not hesitate to ask me
The aircraft is ready for boarding
International newspaper
May I escort you to
Security check
May I introduce

Mr. Park: First class passenger | **Ms. Park**: smile airlines concierge
Ms. Lee: smile airlines lounge representative | **Ms. Bennet**: Flight attendant

Ms. Park Good afternoon Mr. Bennet! I am Ms. Park your concierge from Smile Airlines.

Mr. Bennet Oh, hello.

Mr. Park Mr. Bennet, may I invite you to our club lounge? You can relax there before your flight departs this afternoon.

Mr. Bennet Yes, that would be fine.

Ms. Park Please follow me. Our club lounge is on the third floor. We can use this escalator.

Mr. Bennet All right.

Ms. Park May I carry your coat or your parcel?

Mr. Bennet Oh, thank you very much.

Ms. Park You are welcome.

(at the escalator) After you Mr. Bennet

(at the top of the escalator) This way please.

(inside the lounge) Mr. Bennet this is Ms. Lee, our club lounge representative. She will look after you.

Ms. Lee Welcome to the club lounge, Mr. Bennet

Mr. Bennet Thank you.

Ms. Lee May I have your boarding pass please? I will register you, Mr. Bennet.

Ms. Park And I will hang up your coat in our cloakroom if you would like.

Mr. Bennet Oh, thank you kindly.

Ms. Park You are welcome. I hope you enjoy our light refreshments here.

I will be back to escort you to the aircraft in approximately 30 minutes. Would that be all right, Mr. Bennet?

Mr. Bennet Terrific.

Ms. Lee Mr. Bennet, may I show you our facilities in the lounge?

Mr. Bennet Yes, I'd appreciate that.

Ms. Lee This way please, Mr. Bennet. We have prepared beverages and light refreshmentsat the bar here. The writing counters are in this room equipped with computer printers and stationery.

Mr. Bennet Oh, very good.

Ms. Lee If you wish to make a phone call, the telephone in this booth is for direct dialing as well as for credit cards. The other phone booths are for coin use, we have coins available at the reception counter. Cards can be purchased around the corner. The fax machine is also available at the reception counter. Toilets are through this door, and the television for news and entertainment programs is on the side board at the far corner. If you wish to stretch your legs, please make use of this comfortable lounge chair.

Mr. Bennet Oh, that sounds good.

Ms. Lee There are variety of international newspapers and magazines for your reading pleasure on this rack. They are also available on the consoles at each lounge divider.

Mr. Bennet, we have seats available in the far

corner smoking section and over here in the non-smoking section, which would you prefer?

Mr. Bennet I think I will go for a comfortable lounge chair.

Ms. Lee Certainly, this way please. Please enjoy our beverages and light refreshments.

Mr. Bennet I will, thank you.

Ms. Lee Mr. Bennet, if there is anything I can do to help, please do not hesitate to contact me. I will inform you when our concierge is here to escort you to the aircraft. We also have a TV monitor over here with the information on flight departure times.

Mr. Bennet Very good. Thank you for your help.

Ms. Lee It is my pleasure, Mr. Bennet.

(after 30 minutes)

Ms. Lee Excuse me, Mr. Bennet, Ms. Park, our concierge is here to escort you to the aircraft whenever you are ready.

Mr. Bennet All right, let's go.

Ms. Lee Mr. Bennet, thank you for choosing Smile Airlines. I hope we have the pleasure of serving you again very soon.

Mr. Bennet Goodbye.

Ms. Park The aircraft is now ready for boarding. May I escort you to the boarding gate, Mr. Bennet?

Mr. Bennet Yes, I would be grateful.

Ms. Park Mr. Bennet, this way please. Mr. Bennet, may I inform you there will be a tight security check before the immigration. Please empty your pockets before going through security. The security officer might need to check your baggage after the x-ray.

Mr. Bennet All right.

Ms. Park Mr. Bennet, our boarding gate number 5 is this way please. May I have your boarding pass and passport please?

Mr. Bennet Here they are.

Ms. Park Thank you Mr. Bennet. I will give your boarding pass and passport to our ground staff for boarding formalities. Would you please wait for a moment?

Thank you for waiting. Please follow me.

Good afternoon Ms. Roberts, may I introduce Mr. Bennet our first class passenger?

Ms. Roberts Welcome to our flight, Mr. Bennet.

Mr. Bennet Thank you.

Ms. Park Mr. Bennet, I will be leaving you now. Once again thank you for flying Smile Airlines. Have an enjoyable flight.

Mr. Bennet Thank you.

항공상식 5 비행기가 공중에 뜨는 까닭은?

B747-400기의 크기는 얼마나 될까? 무게는 얼마나 될까? 엄청나게 크고 무거운 비행기가 어떻게 가볍게 공중을 날 수 있을까?

우선 크기를 보면 B747-400기의 앞부분에서 꼬리날개까지 길이는 70.7m로 요즈음 TV에서 자주 보는 농구 코트 길이28m의 2.5배가 넘는다. 또 양 날개 끝의 길이는 64.9m이고 꼬리 날개의 높이는 19.06m로 아파트 약 6층 높이가 된다.

B747-400기의 최대 이륙중량은 약 4백톤에 달한다. 이렇게 거대한 물체가 어떻게 공중에 가볍게 떠오르는 것일까? 지구에 공기가 없다면 어떤 생물체도 살 수 없고 비행기도 날 수가 없다. 비행기는 반드시 공기가 있어야 날 수가 있다. 그래서 비행기는 대류권 밖으로 날 수가 없다.

비행기가 공중에 뜨는 이유를 설명하려면 에어포일Airfoil, 베르누이의 원리Bernoillis principle, 받음각Angle of attack 및 에어플로Airflow가 어쩌고 하면서 양력, 중력, 추력, 항력 관계를 설명하면 너무 머리가 아플 것 같아 여기서는 베르누이 원리와 양력의 기본공식 하나만 인용하고 싶다.

르누이는 스위스 과학자로 벤투리관을 흐르는 공기는 속도가 증가하면 압력이 감소하고 속도가 감소하면 압력이 증가한다는 원리를 발견했다. 이것이 베르누이의 원리이다. 이를 날개에 적용해 간단히 설명하면 날개 위를 지나가는 공기의 속도는 증가해 압력이 낮아지고 반대로 날개 밑으로 지나가는 공기의 속도는 낮아져 압력이 증가하게 돼 비행기는 날개 위와 밑의 차이에 의해 뜨게 되는 것이다.

비행기를 타 본 경험이 있고 호기심이 있는 사람이라면 비행기가 이착륙할 때 날개 끝에서 어떤 것이 길게 나와 날개면적을 크게 하는 것을 보았을 것이다. 이때 날개 끝에서 나오는 것을 플랩Flap이라 하는데 이는 양력을 높이기 위한 장치로 고양력장치라 한다. 플랩을 내리면 날개 모양이 바뀌어 양력계수가 높아지고 날개면적이 넓어져 양력이 증가하므로 낮은 속도에서 이착륙이 가능해진다.

4백톤에 가까운 거대한 B747-400가 뜨는 이유는 날개에서 생기는 양력에 의한 것이며 양력은 공기만이 만들어 낼 수 있는 마술이기도 하다.

Unit 3

Boarding gate

Situation 1 Boarding announcement

• ***words and phrases***

Welcome to Smile Airlines flight
Extend pre-boarding courtesies
We invite
Board at their leisure
We kindly request
Please proceed to gate 4 for boarding
This is the final call for
Smile Airlines paging
Please contact our smile airlines staff at

1. Pre-boarding announcement

Good morning ladies and gentlemen. Welcome to Smile Airlines flight 18 bound for San Francisco. At this time, please remain comfortably seated. Boarding will begin in just a few moments. To avoid congestion, we will be boarding through gate number 5 and would like to extend pre-boarding courtesies to families with small children or infants, or other passengers requiring a little more time or assistance in boarding. We invite our first and executive class passengers to board at their leisure.

2. General boarding announcement 1

Boarding by seat number

Ladies and gentlemen.

Thank you for waiting. Smile Airlines flight 18 bound for San Francisco is now ready for passenger boarding. Passengers seated from rows 34 to 53, please board through gate number 5 at this time.

In addition, may we kindly request all passengers to have their boarding passes available for the staff at the gate.

We invite First and Business class passengers to board at their leisure.

Thank you for flying Smile Airlines and have a nice trip.

Open boarding

Ladies and gentlemen.

Thank you for waiting. Smile Airlines flight 18 bound for San Francisco is now ready for passenger boarding through gate number 5. We kindly request all passengers to have their boarding passes available for the staff at the gate. Thank you for flying Smile Airlines, and we wish you a very pleasant flight.

3. General boarding announcement 2

Boarding by seat number

Thank you for waiting, ladies and gentlemen. We would like to continue boarding Smile Airlines flight number 20 bound for Seattle. All passengers seated in rows 42 to 65 are kindly requested to board the aircraft at this time.
Thank you for flying Smile Airlines, and have a pleasant flight.

Open boarding

May I have your attention please. Smile Airlines flight number 20 bound for Seattle is available for passenger boarding at this time. May we kindly request all confirmed passengers on this flight, please proceed to gate number 4 with boarding passes. Thank you for choosing Smile Airlines today.

4. Final boarding announcement

May I have your attention please. This will be the final call for Smile Airlines flight number 20 bound for Seattle. May we kindly request all remaining passengers, please board the aircraft at this time. Again, we thank you for choosing Smile Airlines and wish you a very pleasant flight.

5. Paging passengers

May I have your attention please. Smile Airlines paging, Mr. Kim Soo-jin departing on Smile Airlines flight 20 to Seattle, please contact a smile airlines staff at the smile airlines information counter located on the 3rd floor. Thank you.

아시아나항공asiana airlines

지난 2000년대 나온 아시아나항공의 "아름다운 사람들" 시리즈 광고이다. 지속적인 홍보 및 광고로 지금은 아시아나항공의 대표 슬로건slogan이 되었다.

Situation 2 Delayed flight announcements

• *words and phrases*

We apologize for the delay in boarding
Current estimated time of departure
ETD
We will keep you advised of any future development
Smile Airlines regrets to announce
We apologize for the continuing delay
Please contact our staff at
We sincerely appreciate your patience and understanding
We would like to offer refreshmentdinnerlunchbreakfast
Compliment of Smile Airlines
Pease accept our apologies

1. Delay announcement 1

Ladies and gentlemen, Smile Airlines would like to apologize for the delay in boarding this morning of flight number 18 bound for New York due to bad weather. Our current estimated time of departure is 11:00AM. May we ask that you remain comfortably seated in the lounge. We will keep you advised of any future developments as soon as we have more information.

2. Delay announcement 2

Ladies and gentlemen, Smile Airlines regrets to announce further delay of flight number 18 bound for New York at this time.

- ✓ the weather is still below the minimum standards for take off.
- ✓ our maintenance crew are still working on the problem.
- ✓ we have still not received clearance from air traffic controllers.

We will give you more information within thirty minutes. Again, we apologize for any inconvenience we may have caused you today. Thank you.

3. Delay announcement 3

Ladies and gentlemen, Smile Airlines would like to apologize for the continuing delay of flight number 18 bound for New York due to bad weather. We are currently estimating a departure time of 8PM. If you are making a connection in New York and you are concerned about your connection, please contact our staff located in front of gate number 7. Again, we apologize for the delay and sincerely appreciate your patience and understanding in this matter.

4. Delay announcement 4

Ladies and gentlemen, Smile Airlines would like to apologize for the continuing delay of flight number 18 bound for New York. We would like to offer all passengers at this time dinner. Please show your boarding pass to any of the snack counters located in the gate area for the meal service, compliments of Smile Airlines. In the meantime, we will continue making announcements every thirty minutes to keep you updated on the situation. Thank you for your patience and again, please accept our apologies.

대한항공korean air

2014년 대한항공에서 선보인 광고이다. 경쟁항공사인 아시아나 항공이 2014년 A380을 도입해 운항을 시작하자, 아시아나항공의 브랜드 컬러인 회색과 대한항공의 브랜드 컬러인 하늘색을 입힌 버스로 대한항공의 A380 좌석 수가 상대적으로 적어 더 쾌적하고 여유로울 수 있다는 부분을 강조하는 경쟁사 비교광고이다.

Situation 3 Boarding gate

• *words and phrases*

General boarding	I will check the availability

1. Normal boarding procedure

Staff May I have your boarding pass please?

Customer Here it is.

Staff Thank you Mr. Brown. Have a pleasant flight.

2. Pre-boarding an elderly passenger

Staff Excuse me, would you like to get on the aircraft before we start general boarding?

Passenger Yes. I suppose that would be helpful.

Staff Certainly sir, may I help you with your hand luggage?

Passenger Oh, thank you, young lady.

Staff Certainly sir, please follow me.

3. Change of seat request

Customer	Excuse me. I have been given a middle seat but I'd prefer a window or an aisle.
Staff	Certainly ma'am, I will check the availability on our computer for you now. We have a window seat number 29A. How would that be?
Customer	Much better, thanks.
Staff	Certainly ma'am. I will change your boarding pass for you now. May I have your old boarding pass? Mrs. Turner, here is your new boarding pass, window seat 29A. I hope you enjoy your flight.
Customer	Many thanks.

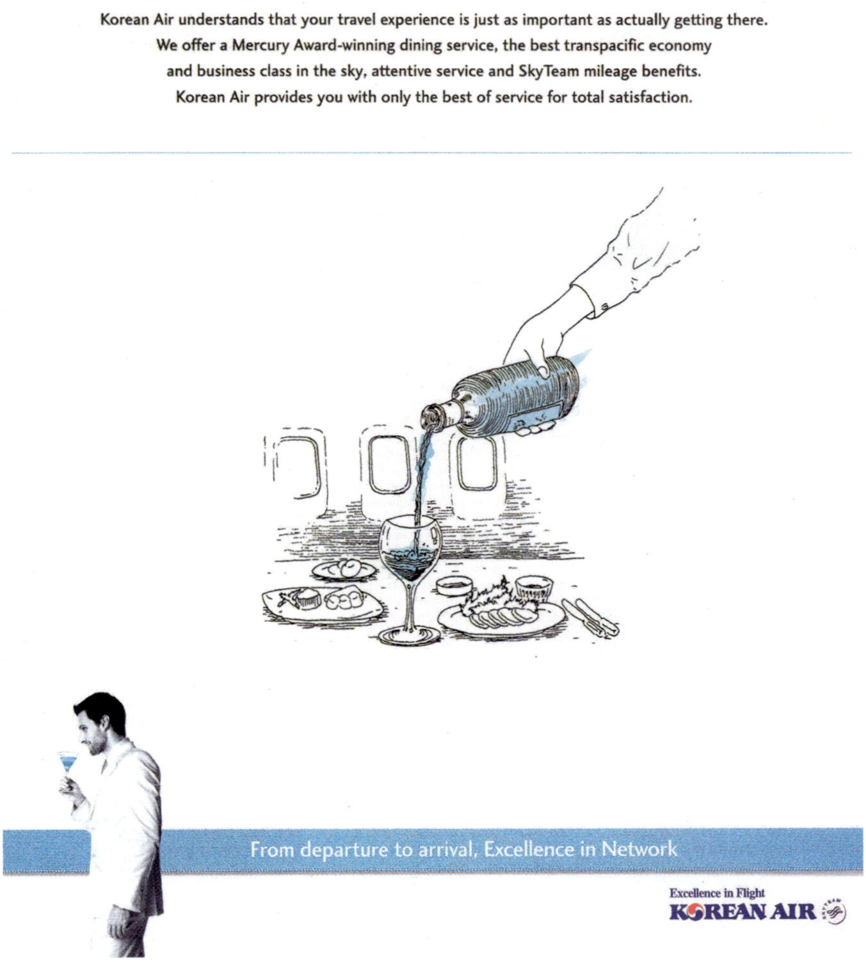

대한항공korean air

세계 최고 수준의 서비스를 제공하는 대한민국 최대의 항공사이며, 아시아의 대형 항공사 중 하나로 인천 국제공항을 중심으로 유럽, 아시아, 오스트레일리아, 북미 등 전 세계를 운항하고 있다. 세계적 디자이너 지안 프랑코 페레가 디자인한 새 유니폼이 고객들에게 좋은 반응을 얻고 있다.

항공상식 6 운항 정시성

항공여행의 최대 이점은 시공을 초월하는 데 있다. 동쪽으로 날아 시간을 앞지르기도 하고 서쪽으로 날면 지구의 자전 속도와도 경쟁을 할 수 있다.

서울에서 오후 5시에 LA로 출발하면 날짜 변경선을 넘어 11시간을 비행하고도 같은 날 정오에 도착하니 5시간을 앞지른 셈이다. 또 서울에서 오후 4시에 출발하여 11시간을 비행한 후 런던에 도착하면 오후 8시, 지구의 자전속도와 무려 7시간 동안 경주를 한 셈이다.

남쪽으로 적도를 넘어서면 호주나 뉴질랜드는 지금 늦가을을 맞고 있다. 계절까지 바꾸어 놓을 수 있는 것이 항공여행인 것이다. 이렇게 시간을 주름잡고 날아다니는 항공기이지만 정작 스케줄을 지키는 정시운항에는 어려움이 적지 않다.

항공편의 출발은 스케줄에서 5분 이내, 도착은 15분 이내일 때 정시운항으로 간주한다. 실제로 항공 여행자들을 대상으로 여론조사 한 것을 보면 항공사의 평가에 가장 중요한 항목으로 꼽는 것이 정시성이다. 다시 말하면 이 정시성이 바로 항공사의 경영능력을 말해주는 바로미터다. 완벽한 정비·예약·탑승수속·지상조업·운항 분야가 정시성을 위해 조직화되고 역량이 집결되지 않으면 좀처럼 이루기 힘든 것이기 때문이다.

미국의 저요금 항공사 중 꾸준한 성장을 거듭하고 있는 사우스웨스트항공은 주력 기종으로 B737 항공기만 2백26대를 보유하고 있는데 어느 공항에서나 도착 후 다음 편 출발시점까지 지상계류시간은 25분으로 스케줄을 운영하고 있다. 나머지 시간은 정비를 제외하고는 모두 공중에 떠있는 셈이다. 이름난 항공사들도 항공편 1회전에 최소 35분에서 40분이 소요된다. 2백26대가 하루에 대당 3왕복에 지상 계류시간을 30분만 줄이면 하루에 총 3백39시간, 1대당 하루 평균 가동시간을 11시간이라고 가정하면 30대의 항공기를 공짜로 보유하고 있는 것과 같은 효과를 얻는다.

시간은 돈이라는 상업적 의미를 운항 정시성은 잘 대변하고 있다고 볼 수 있다.

Unit 4

Arrival service

Situation 1 Passenger message

• ***words and phrases***

Message
You will see a phone
Would you like to come with me please?
Tight connection
I hope we have the pleasure of serving you again
Transfer desk
Mishandling
I will do my best to
Unaccompanied baggage
Authorization
Let me explain what I can do
When is the best time
We do take full responsibility
Central baggage service office

Mr. Philip: Passenger

Ms. Park: Smile arrival staff with a sign board for messages

Ms. Park	Good evening sir. How may I help you?
Mr. Philip	My name is Ron Philip. I believe you have a message for me.
Ms. Park	Certainly Mr. Philip. May I see your passport or boarding pass please?
Mr. Philip	Here you are.
Ms. Park	Thank you Mr. Philip, here is your message.
Mr. Philip	Thanks. Can you tell me where I can find a phone?
Ms. Park	Certainly, go straight ahead and you will see a phone on your right. Immigration is directly beyond.
Mr. Philip	Many thanks.
Ms. Park	You are welcome, Mr. Philip.

Situation 2 Tight connection time

Ms. Carter: Passenger | **Mr. Wun**: *smile airlines staff*

Mr. Wun Welcome to seoul ma'am, how may I help you?

Ms. Carter I'm connecting to a Thai flight that leaves in 45 minutes.

Mr. Wun Certainly ma'am. May I ask your connecting flight number?

Ms. Carter Yes, here is my ticket. Ah, it's Thai flight 12 departing at 1:50PM.

Mr. Wun I see you have a very tight connection Ms. Carter. Would you like to come with me please.
I'll take you to the Thai counter at the transfer desk. Is your luggage checked through to your final destination, Ms. Carter?

Ms. Carter Yes it is.

Mr. Wun Fine, please follow me and we will get you checked-in.

At the Counter

Mr. Wun	Ms. Carter, the Thai staff here will look after you now.
Ms. Carter	Oh, thank you for your help.
Mr. Wun	It was my pleasure. I hope we have the pleasure of serving you on Smile Airlines again.

Situation 3 Lost luggage

Mr. Choi: smile airlines staff | **Mrs. Lane**: Passenger

Mr. Choi Good afternoon, how may I help you?

Mrs. Lane My bags have not arrived yet.

Mr. Choi I'm sorry. May I have your ticket and baggage claim tags, please?

Mrs. Lane Here they are.

Mr. Choi How many bags did you check-in Mrs. Lane?

Mrs. Lane Two.

Mr. Choi Did either one arrive?

Mrs. Lane No.

Mr. Choi Please wait here. I will go to see if all bags have come off the plane.

Mrs. Lane Alright.

(After 5 minutes)

Mr. Choi I am very sorry Mrs. Lane. I did not find your bags.

Mrs. Lane Where could they be?

Mr. Choi Mrs. Lane, I apologize for the mishandling of your bags. I will do my best to get them to you as soon as possible.

Mrs. Lane This is terrible!

Mr. Choi I do understand your frustration. Let me explain what I can do for you. First, we will fill out the unaccompanied baggage authorization form for Korean customs (fill in form address / phone etc.) Thank you, may I have your passport and tickets please?

Mrs. Lane Here.

Mr. Choi Thank you. I see you flew from Taipei to Tokyo on smile airlines flight 20 and then connected to smile airlines flight 21 to Seoul, is that correct?

Mrs. Lane Yes.

Mr. Choi Which pictures look like your bags?

Mrs. Lane These ones.

Mr. Choi And the color?

Mrs. Lane They are both black.

Mr. Choi Do you have name tags on your bags?

Mrs. Lane Yes.

Mr. Choi Mrs. Lane, were the bags locked?

Mrs. Lane No.

Mr. Choi Fine, Mrs. Lane, we will start tracking your bags immediately. Usually most bags are found and arrive the next day.

Mrs. Lane I should hope so.

Mr. Choi As well, if necessary we will contact you everyday for four days to let you know what is happening. I see you are staying at the Holiday Inn Hotel, telephone number 6383-2454, is that correct?

Mrs. Lane Yes.

Mr. Choi When is the best time to contact you?

Mrs. Lane Early morning or after 7:00PM.

Mr. Choi Certainly. In the rare case that your bags are not found after 4 days, your file will be forwarded to our central baggage service office in Chicago. Let me assure you Mrs. Lane, we do take full responsibility for your bags.

Mrs. Lane I understand.

Mr. Choi My name is Mr. Choi. Please feel free to contact me at any time.

Mrs. Lane Thank you for your help.

Situation 4 Misplaced bags

Mr. Choi: smile airlines staff | **Mrs. Green**: Passenger

Mr. Choi Good afternoon, how may I help you?

Mrs. Green I've been waiting for my luggage and it has not come down yet. I'm worried that it may have been lost. Everyone else has claimed their bags but mine are missing.

Mr. Choi I am sorry to hear that. May I see your ticket and baggage claim tags please?

Mrs. Green Yes, here they are.

Mr. Choi Mrs. Green. I see that you checked-in 2 pieces of baggage. Did either of them arrive?

Mrs. Green No, neither one.

Mr. Choi Would you mind if I go to look and check that all bags have been taken off the plane?

Mrs. Green Should I wait here?

Mr. Choi Yes, I will be back in 5 minutes.

(After 5 minutes)

Mr. Choi I am very sorry Mrs. Green, it looks like your bags did not make it on this flight.

Mrs. Green What do you mean? Where could they be?

Mr. Choi Mrs. Green, on behalf of Smile Airlines I would like to sincerely apologize for mishandling your bags. I will do my utmost to make sure they are returned to you.

Mrs. Green But, I need my samples for an important meeting the day after tomorrow. Without them, my trip will be a total waste.

Mr. Choi I do understand that you have important materials in your bags. Let me explain what needs to be done now in order that we may have this process start as soon as possible. First, we need to fill out "unaccompanied baggage authorization form" for Korean customs. This allows us to clear your baggage on your behalf when it does arrive.

Mrs. Green Oh, I am so upset!

Mr. Choi I will do everything possible to get your bags to you before your meeting. Mrs. Green, may I see your passport and ticket please?

Thank you.

I see you checked-in 2 bags at Vancouver, Canadian Airlines flight 7 connecting at Seattle to Smile Airlines flight 20 to Seoul. Is that correct?

Mrs. Green Yes. it was a very tight connection in Seattle.

Mr. Choi It is possible that the problem occurred there. Which of these pictures looks most like your baggage?

Mrs. Green This one with the wheels.

Mr. Choi Which of these colors is closest to the color of your baggage?

Mrs. Green One is black and the other is blue.

Mr. Choi Do you have name tags attached to your bags? Do they it have your name and your home address on them?

Mrs. Green Yes, my name and address were on the bags.

Mr. Choi Is your baggage locked?

Mrs. Green No.

Mr. Choi Are there any distinguishing marks on the bags that could help us to identify your baggage?

Mrs. Green Yes, the black one has an "I love Hawaii" sticker on it and the blue one has some red paint on the handle.

Mr. Choi Oh, I'll write that down. That may help us locate your bags. Mrs. Green, let me assure you that tracking efforts will begin immediately with our computerized tracking system. All bags that fit your luggage description, both within the smile airlines system and all other major carriers worldwide, will be checked and then forwarded to Korea on the first available flight. Our experience has shown that over 95% of all missing bags arrive the next day.

Mrs. Green Oh, really? That makes me feel better.

Mr. Choi In addition, a representative from Smile Airlines will contact you every day, for the first four days, if the bag has been found, to keep you apprised of the situation.

Mrs. Green, let me confirm that you are staying at the West in Hotel in Seoul and that your contact number is 345-4567. Is that correct?

Mrs. Green Yes.

Mr. Choi What is the best time to contact you?

Mrs. Green I will be at the hotel between 4 and 6PM everyday.

Mr. Choi Fine. In the rare event that even after 96 hours our local office has been unable to locate your baggage, a copy of your file will be forwarded to our central baggage service office in Chicago. This department will then use it's extensive tracking capabilities with all other carriers in an effort to locate your luggage.

In any event, we will take full responsibility for this case until the baggage is found or a fair compensation has been made.

Mrs. Green I understand.

Mr. Choi And finally, we've prepared this "we're sorry"

	brochure that gives you a written explanation of what I've just said, phone number for our office along with the operating hours, and a copy of the claim form for your records.
Mrs. Green	Ok.
Mr. Choi	Mrs. Green, please allow me to escort you through customs so I can explain the situation to them.

(After Customs)

Mr. Choi	Again Mrs. Green, I apologize for this inconvenience and hope that this will in no way deter you from using Smile Airlines again in the future.
Mrs. Green	Mr. Choi, thank you for your help.

Situation 5 Telephone courtesy

• *words and phrases*

I'm sorry	Our requested seat is not available
May I offer you	It is possible
At the last moment	In addition
You are welcome	

Mrs. Ford: Passenger | **Mr. Jin**: smile airlines staff

Mr. Jin Good morning, Smile Airlines passenger service. This is Mr. Jin speaking. How may I help you?

Mrs. Ford Oh, hello, I was on your flight from Tokyo last night and I left my glasses in the seat pocket.

Mr. Jin Oh, I see.

Mrs. Ford Have any glasses been turned into your lost and found?

Mr. Jin I am sorry ma'am, it will take me a few minutes to check that for you. May I call back in 15 minutes?

Mrs. Ford Yes, of course.

Mr. Jin Thank you. May I have your name and telephone number, please?

Mrs. Ford Yes, my name is Mrs. Ford and my telephone number is 555-5678.

Mr. Jin	May I ask you to spell your name please ma'am.
Mrs. Ford	Yes, it's f-o-r-d.
Mr. Jin	Thank you, Mrs. Ford and your phone number is 555-5678. You left your glasses on our flight from Tokyo last night. Would that have been flight 60, Mrs. Ford?
Mrs. Ford	Yes. That's right.
Mr. Jin	Mrs. Ford, can you describe your glasses to me?
Mrs. Ford	They have red rims and were in a black leather case.
Mr. Jin	Red rims in the black leather case, certainly Mrs. Ford. I will phone you back in 15 minutes and let you know if they were turned in. Would that be alright?

(After 15 minutes)

Mr. Jin	Good morning. Is Mrs. Ford there please?
Mr. Ford	This is Mrs. Ford.
Mr. Jin	This is Mr. Jin from Smile Airlines. I'm pleased to tell you we have your glasses. One of our cleaning staff turned them in.
Mrs. Ford	Oh, I'm so relieved. Thank you so much.
Mr. Jin	Mrs. Ford, you are welcome. What is the best way to deliver your glasses to you?

Mrs. Ford Actually, I will be at the airport tomorrow. Can I pick them up at your office?

Mr. Jin Yes, certainly. You will find our office in room 1543 of the airport terminal building on the 4th floor.

Mrs. Ford Fine, and thank you for your help.

Mr. Jin Mrs. Ford, it was my pleasure. I'm so glad we found your glasses.

Mrs. Ford Good bye.

Mr. Jin Good bye.

항공상식 7

항공기 내 첨단시설물

첨단화되어가는 기내 오락물을 이용해 보자.

몇 주 동안 파도를 가르며 바다를 항해하는 여객선은 수영장을 비롯한 각종 스포츠 및 오락시설을 갖추고 있으며 갑판에 올라가서 바람을 쏘일 수도 있다.

그러나 여객기는 속도가 빨라 12시간이면 태평양을 횡단할 수 있는 반면, 비행 중에는 창문을 열 수 없는 완전히 밀폐된 공간이기 때문에 여객선보다 훨씬 더 무료하다.

그래서 여객기는 그 특성에 맞는 각종 오락 시스템을 갖추어 비행중의 무료함을 조금이라도 덜어주려고 노력하고 있다.

여객기에 이러한 오락시스템이 도입된 것은 생각보다 그 역사가 오래다. 1929년 미국의 트랜스 컨티넨탈 항공사가 여객기의 객실에서 뉴스와 만화를 상영한 것이 기내 영화의 시초였고 1970년대에 대형기가 취항하면서 시네마스코프를 연상케 하는 대형 스크린을 갖춘 기내영화가 등장했다.

최근 정보화 시대를 맞이하여 여객기의 객실에서도 이제는 인공위성을 이용한 디지털화된 신시스템이나 컴퓨터화된 기내 오락시스템이 도입되어 그만큼 서비스가 다양해졌다. 특히 이러한 시스템은 좌석마다 장착됨으로써 승객들이 좌석에 앉아서 개인전용의 전화·음악·텔레비전·영화·게임에 이르기까지 각종 새로운 서비스를 이용하거나 즐길 수 있다.

기내 전화 서비스가 도입되면서 태평양 상공을 비행하면서 승객들은 서울의 친지에게 연락은 물론, 도착지 호텔이나 식당 예약도 할 수 있다. 또한 각 좌석마다 전원장치가 장착되어 이곳에 어댑터를 꽂으면 자동차 안에서처럼 노트북PC를 사용할 수 있을 뿐더러 인터넷 접속까지도 가능해 사무실에서 하던 일을 그대로 할 수 있게 됐다.

영화가 상영되지 않을 때는 목적지에 도착할 때까지의 비행정보를 스크린에 시각적으로 알려주는 새로운 시스템을 도입하여 비행 중에 승객들이 가장 궁금해 하는 현재의 비행 위치를 지도상에 보여주고 비행속도·고도·외부온도와 도착 예정시간 등을 알려준다. 한편 이런 첨단 기내시설물들은 승객들에게 즐거움을 주기도 하지만 일에 시달리는 비즈니스맨들에게는 비행시간 동안이나마 쉬거나 잠을 청하는 기회를 박탈당하게 되는 아쉬움도 있다.

Section 5

IN-FLIGHT SERVICE

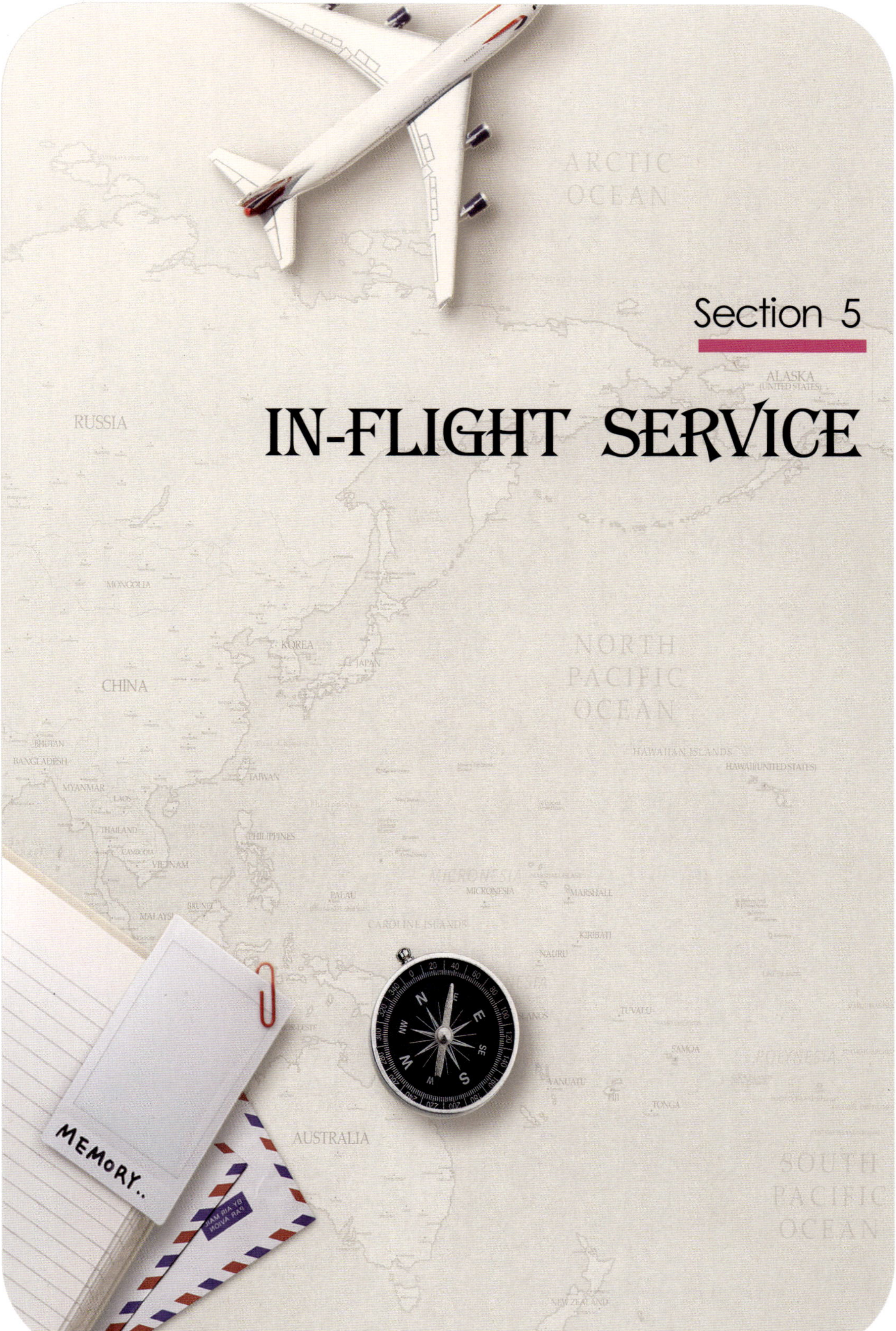

Objectives

To expand your English vocabulary in airline industry.

To role-play various In-flight service situations with a focus on appropriate service English.

To practice using polite and positive English to deal with demanding passenger situations.

To understand the role of Flight Attendants.

To develop communication skills to meet and exceed the needs of English speaking customers.

To learn Airline Service procedures.

To learn to manage stress, and overcome difficult situations.

To be competent and confident in using Airline Service English.

Unit 1

In-flight announcement

1. Flight information

Ladies and gentlemen.

This is Smile Airlines flight 10, bound for Los Angeles.

While you are getting comfortable in the cabin this is a reminder that all carry-on baggage must fit securely either in the overhead bins or directly under the seat in front of you. Prior to closing the aircraft door we must verify that all passengers are seated and that all carry-on bags are stowed. Thank you for your Cooperation.

안내 말씀드리겠습니다.
저희 비행기는 LA까지 가는 스마일 항공 010편입니다. 출발 전에 탑승 편수를 다시 한번 확인해 주시기 바랍니다.
그리고 손님 여러분의 안전하고 편안한 여행을 위해 가지고 계신 짐들은 위쪽 보관함에 넣어 주시고, 깨지기 쉬운 물건 등은 앞좌석 밑에 넣어주시기 바랍니다.
아울러 보관함을 여실 때는 먼저 넣은 다른 짐들이 떨어지지 않도록 유의해 주시기 바랍니다.
탑승이 완료되는 대로 출발하도록 하겠습니다.
감사합니다.

2. Welcome

Good morning ladies and gentlemen.

We would like to welcome you on board Smile Airlines flight 10 bound for Los Angeles.

The captain of this flight is Soohyun Yoon and this is Jisoo Kim, your flight attendant.

Today's flight time will be 11 hours and 30 minutes following take-off.

Other personal electronic devices should not be switched on until 15 minutes after take-off and must be switched off when the fasten seat belt sign comes on for landing.

Our captain will provide you with more flight information after take-off.

Before our departure, please make sure that your seat back is in the upright position and tray tables are closed.

Also, please, refrain from smoking at all times during the flight.

The use of portable phones, citizens band radios are not allowed at any time.

Your cooperation will be much appreciated.

If there is anything we can do for you, please let us know.

We wish you a pleasant flight. Thank you.

손님 여러분, 안녕하십니까?
저희 스마일 항공을 탑승해 주셔서 감사합니다.
저희 비행기는 LA까지 가는 스마일 항공 10편입니다. LA까지 여러분을 모실 기장은 윤수현이며 저는 객실 승무원 김지수입니다.
LA까지의 비행시간은 11시간 30분으로 예정하고 있으며, 기타 운항에 관한 자세한 사항은 이륙 후 다시 기장의 안내가 있을 예정입니다. 지금부터 안전을 위해 좌석 벨트를 매주시고 좌석 등받이와 테이블을 제자리로 해 주십시오.
쾌적한 항공 여행을 위해 저희 스마일 항공에서는 전 노선 금연을 실시하고 있으며, 특히 화장실에서의 흡연은 항공법으로 금지된 사항이니 협조해 주시기 바랍니다.
항공기 안전 운항에 저해가 되는 휴대용 전화기, 디지털 카메라, FM/AM 라디오 등의 전자제품은 탑승 시부터 도착 후 내리실 때까지 계속해서 사용하실 수 없습니다. 지금 확인하시고 전원을 꺼 주시기 바랍니다.
여행 중 도움이 필요하시면 언제든지 저희 승무원을 불러주십시오.
LA까지 저희 스마일 항공과 함께 편안한 여행이 되시기 바랍니다.
감사합니다.

말레이시아항공malaysia airlines

동남아 최대 항공사 중 하나인 말레이시아항공은 세계 최고 수준의 기내 서비스로 정평이 나 있으며, 최근에는 영국의 스카이트랙스skytrax가 선정한 5 Star 항공사에 선정되기도 했다.

3. Demonstration

Ladies and gentlemen.

We would like to familiarize you with the safety features of this aircraft.

Please, pay attention to the following video demonstration.

Thank you.

손님 여러분. 지금부터 안전에 관한 Video를 상영하겠습니다.
앞쪽의 화면에 주목해 주시기 바랍니다. 감사합니다.

4. Take off

Ladies and gentlemen.

We will be taking off immediately.

Please make sure that your seatbelt is fastened.

Thank you.

손님 여러분, 저희 비행기는 곧 이륙하겠습니다.
좌석 벨트의 착용 상태를 다시 한번 확인해 주시기 바랍니다.
감사합니다.

5. Seatbelt sign off

Ladies and gentlemen.

Although the seatbelt sign has been turned off, we recommend that you continue to fastened your seatbelt during the flight.

Thank you.

손님 여러분, 지금부터 좌석 벨트 착용 표시등이 꺼져 이동하실 수 있습니다만, 갑작스러운 기체의 흔들림에 대비해 가급적 이동을 삼가해 주시고 좌석에 앉아 계실 때는 안전을 위해 계속해서 좌석 벨트를 착용하시기 바랍니다. 감사합니다.

6. Cabin service

Ladies and gentlemen.

This is your flight attendant. Jisoo Kim.

For your comfort and safety, there are 17 flight attendants on board today.

If you need any assistance, please contact your flight attendant.

Now I would like to tell you about our services for today's flight.

In a few minutes, we'll be serving cocktails and soft drinks followed by lunch.

Duty free sales will follow after the meal service.

And then 2 movies will be presented for your entertainment.

2 hours before arrival, snacks will be served.

For further details on service procedures, please refer to your in-flight magazine, on page 21. We wish you a pleasant flight.

Thank you.

손님 여러분, 안녕하십니까? 저는 객실 승무원 김지수입니다.
오늘 손님 여러분의 편안하고 안전한 여행을 위해 저희 객실에는 17명의 객실 승무원이 탑승하고 있습니다.
여행 중 도움이 필요하시면 언제든지 담당 승무원을 불러주시기 바랍니다.
잠시 후, 각종 칵테일을 포함한 음료와 식사를 제공해 드리고 식사 후에는 면세품 판매가 있겠습니다.
2편의 영화를 상영해 드리고 도착 시간 전에 간단한 음료와 식사를 다시 제공해 드릴 예정입니다.
보다 자세한 내용은 좌석 앞 주머니 속의 기내지 21page를 참고하시기 바랍니다.
감사합니다.

7. Duty free sales

Ladies and gentlemen.

In a few minutes, we'll begin our sales of duty free items.

If you'd like to purchase any items, please let us know as the duty free cart passes by your seat.

We accept Korean Won, US Dollars and Japanese Yen… and credit card.

The duty free allowances for the United States are 1liter(s) of liquor, 2 packs of cigarettes and 4 ounces of perfume.

For further information, please contact your flight attendants.

Thank you.

안내 말씀드리겠습니다.
저희 기내에서는 필요하신 분들을 위해 다양한 면세품을 일반 면세점보다 저렴한 가격에 판매하고 있습니다.
잠시 후, 면세품 판매를 시작할 예정이니 구입을 원하시는 손님께서는 저희 면세품 판매대가 지나갈 때 구입하시기 바랍니다.
면세품 구입 시 지불하실 수 있는 화폐는 한국 원, 미국 달러, 일본 엔 그리고 신용카드입니다.
참고로, 미국에 입국하시는 손님의 면세 허용량은 주류 1병(또는 리터), 담배 2보루, 향수 4온스입니다.
감사합니다.

8. Movie

Ladies and gentlemen.

In a few minutes, We'll be showing you a movie titled Love Story.

Please turn to channel 2 for English and channel 11 for Korean.

Snacks and refreshments are available at all times.

We hope you enjoy our movie.

Thank you.

손님 여러분, 잠시 후 영화를 상영해 드리겠습니다.
오늘 여러분께서 보실 영화는 러브 스토리입니다.
한국어는 CHANNEL 11, 영어는 CHANNEL 2에서 들으실 수 있습니다.(그리고 영화를 감상하시는 동안 간단한 간식을 제공해 드리겠습니다.)
즐거운 시간이 되시기 바랍니다.
감사합니다.

9. Documentation

1) *Korea*

Ladies and gentlemen, for entering Korea, please have your passport and entry documents ready.
For further information, please contact your flight attendant.
Thank you.

손님 여러분, 입국에 필요한 서류를 확인해 주시기 바랍니다.
입국 시 제출하실 서류는 입국신고서, 세관신고서, 검역신고서가 있습니다.
서류 작성 시 문의 사항이 있으시면 저희 승무원을 불러주시기 바랍니다.
감사합니다.

2) *Japan*

All passengers must fill out the immigration form.
Passengers who have items over the limit of duty free allowance must also fill out the customs form.

입국신고서는 모든 분이 작성하셔야 하며, 세관신고서는 면세 범위를 초과한 휴대품을 가지고 계신 분만 작성하시기 바랍니다.

3) *The United States*

The United States government requires that an immigration form must be completed by all passengers, except US citizens, Canadian citizens, US green card holders, and passengers with US immigrant visas.

All nationalities must fill out the US customs form before entering the Untied States. Families traveling together only need to fill out one form.

Also, passengers having more than 10,000 US dollars or the equivalent amount in foreign currency or traveler's checks must declare the amount on the form.

Those passengers with connecting flights are also required to pick up all checked baggage and clear customs here in Los Angeles before your next flight.

미국시민, 영주권 소지자, 최초 이민승객, 캐나다 시민권 소지자를 제외한 모든 분께서는 반드시 입국신고서를 작성하시고, 세관신고서는 가족당 한 매만 작성하시면 됩니다.
그리고 미화 만 불 이상 또는 이에 해당하는 외화를 소지하신 분께서는 반드시 세관신고서에 기재 후 신고하시기 바랍니다.
그리고 과일, 야채, 동식물류 등의 물품을 가지고 계신 분께서도 반드시 신고하시기 바랍니다.
또한, 도착 후 계속해서 다른 항공편으로 여행하시는 손님께서는 반드시 이곳 LA에서 짐을 찾아 세관 검사를 받으시기 바랍니다.

10. Approach

Ladies and gentlemen.

We are now making our descent into Los Angeles.

At this time we request that you return to your seat and fasten your seatbelt.

Please make sure your bags are stowed properly in either the overhead bins or under the seat.

And please turn off all personal electronic devices.

Your flight attendants will be collecting earphones shortly.

We hope you enjoyed your flight.

Thank you for your assistance.

손님 여러분, 저희 비행기는 약 30분 후에 LA 국제공항에 도착하겠습니다.
좌석에 앉으셔서 좌석 벨트를 착용해 주시고 꺼내놓으신 짐들은 출발할 때의 위치에 다시 보관해 주십시오.
그리고 사용하시던 모든 전자제품의 전원을 꺼주시기 바랍니다.
지금부터, 착륙 준비를 위해 손님 여러분께서 사용하시던 헤드폰을 회수하겠습니다.
감사합니다.

11. Landing

Ladies and gentlemen.

We are now making our final approach into Los Angeles.

Please make sure that your seatbelt is fastened, return your seat back to its upright position and your tray table is closed.

Thank you.

손님 여러분, 저희 비행기는 곧 착륙하겠습니다.
좌석 벨트의 착용 상태를 다시 한번 확인해 주시고 좌석 등받이와 테이블은 원래의 위치로 되돌려 주시기 바랍니다.
감사합니다.

전일본공수all nippon airways

아나ANA항공은 일본항공과 함께 일본의 대표적인 항공사 중 하나이다. 아나항공은 대외적으로는 일본인 특유의 친절과 안전의식을 중시하는 기업, 대내적으로는 자유롭고 가족적인 분위기의 기업이라는 이미지를 가지고 있다. 세계 유수의 항공서비스 관련 언론으로부터 최고의 서비스 제공 항공사로 선정되는 등 전문가 그룹 및 승객들에게 좋은 반응을 받고 있는 항공사이다.

12. Transit information

Ladies and gentlemen.

For passengers connecting with domestic flights today, please complete entry forms and contact the Airline Information desk located in the arrival area.

Those passengers continuing onto another international flight, please follow the guidance of our ground staff.

If you have any questions please let us know.

Thank you.

그리고 LA 국제공항에 도착 후, 계속해서 국내선을 이용하시는 손님께서는 내리셔서 모든 짐을 찾아 세관 검사를 받으신 후, 도착장 1층에 있는 항공사 도착 안내 카운터에서 국내선 연결 서비스를 받으시기 바랍니다. 그리고, 계속해서 국제선 연결 편을 이용하시는 손님께서는 내리셔서 저희 공항직원의 안내를 받으신 후 통과 여객 대합실에서 휴식을 취하시기 바랍니다. 감사합니다.

13. Farewell

Ladies and gentlemen.

We have just landed at LA International airport. The local time is 10:00AM.

For your safety, we request that you remain seated until the aircraft has come to a complete stop at the terminal and the seatbelt sign has turned off.

Before deplaning please make sure that you have all your personal belongings with you.

On behalf of Smile Airlines we would like to thank you for allowing us to serve you today and we hope to see you again.

손님 여러분, 저희 스마일 항공과 함께 즐겁고 편안한 여행이 되셨습니까?
저희 비행기는 방금 LA 공항에 착륙했습니다.
이곳 현지 시각은 4월 5일 오전 10시입니다.
손님 여러분의 안전을 위해 비행기가 완전히 멈춘 후 저희 승무원이 안내해 드릴 때까지 좌석에서 잠시만 기다려 주시기 바랍니다.
내리실 때는 잊으신 물건이 없는지 다시 한번 확인하시고 머리 위 보관함을 여실 때는 물건이 떨어지지 않도록 유의해 주시기 바랍니다.
저희 스마일 항공은 더욱 안전하고 정성스럽게 여러분을 모실 것을 약속드리며, 오늘 스마일 항공을 이용해 주신 손님 여러분께 다시 한번 감사드립니다.

14. Deplane

Ladies and gentlemen.

You may now exit through the forward door.

Please allow those passengers seated in front of you to exit first.

Passengers seated in the back of the aircraft,

please exit through the rear door.

Thank you. Good bye.

손님 여러분, 지금부터 앞문을 이용해 내려주시기 바랍니다.
객실 뒤편에 계신 손님께서는 좌석에서 잠시만 기다려 주십시오.(그리고 객실 뒤편에 계신 손님께서는 뒷문을 이용해 주시기 바랍니다.)
감사합니다. 안녕히 가십시오.

항공상식 8

항공기 화장실 궁금하지요?

장거리를 다니는 우등 고속버스에 화장실이 없어 승객들이 많은 불편을 겪고 있다. 용변이 급한 사람들은 참다 참다 휴게소에 들러 달라고 운전기사에게 부탁을 해야 한다. 이런 사태는 비행기가 처음 등장했을 때도 발생했다.

조종사만 타던 비행기에서 승객을 실어 나르기 시작한 초창기 여객기 시대만 해도 지금과 같은 별실의 화장실은 없었고 빈통을 기내 뒤 구석에 두고 변기 대신으로 사용했다.

1930년대말 근대 여객기 DC4가 등장하면서 처음으로 독립된 화장실이 생겼으나 변기는 이동식을 채용했기 때문에 여객기가 공항에 도착하면 변기를 들어내 청소해야 하는 불편이 있었다. 그러다 1945년에 취항한 더글러스사의 장거리 여객기 DC 6B는 탱크식의 고정식 변기를 처음으로 설치하여 공항에 도착한 뒤 오물 청소차가 와서 변기를 청소하는 형식으로 바뀌었다.

이 화장실은 제트여객기가 등장하면서부터 호텔 수준으로 변했다. 변기가 본격적인 수세식으로 바뀌었으며 화장실 내의 비품도 전기면도용 소켓·간단한 화장품 등 마치 호텔의 화장실을 연상케 할 정도로 화려해졌다. 이 수세식 화장실은 순환식으로 사용한 물을 여과하여 깨끗이 한 후 비행 중에 몇 번이고 다시 화장실용 물로 사용한다. 물론 살균·탈취·착색 등 엄격한 위생처리를 하고 있다. 그렇다고 세면대 물도 순환이 되는 것은 아니다. B747-400과 같은 최신 여객기들은 화장실이 수세식이 아니고 공기 흡입식이다.

혹시 이 기종을 탑승할 기회가 되어 화장실을 이용할 경우 변기에 앉아서 플러시 버튼을 누르면 엉덩이가 변기에 빨려 내려갈까? 이러한 염려를 불식시키기 위하여 변기 앉는 부분의 밑부분에 홈을 만들어 공기가 들어가도록 만들어 놓았다.

그럼 항공기에는 화장실이 몇 개나 있나? B747-400의 경우는 14개, MD-11은 9개, A300은 7개의 화장실이 있다.

일반적으로 일등석에는 10인당 1개, 일반석에는 35인당 1개를 기준으로 화장실을 설치한다. 대한항공의 경우에는 중장거리용 항공기에 여성 전용 화장실을 장착해 운용하고 있는데 점보기에는 3개, 중형기에는 2개의 여성 전용 화장실을 설치하고 있다.

이 여성 전용 화장실은 내부 벽지를 핑크빛 꽃무늬 벽지를 사용하여 화사하게 꾸며 여성 전용 공간임을 연출하고 화장실 내에 비치되는 여러 화장품도 여성 전용으로 교체하였다.

Unit 2

In the cabin

1. Boarding

Situation 1 At the boarding gate

• *words and phrases*

welcome aboard	boarding pass
take-off	landing
assistance	aisle
here is your seat	in the front of the cabin
in the middle of the cabin	in the back of the cabin
take the other aisle	

would you mind keeping your bags under the seat in front of you

FA: Flight attendant | **P**: Passenger

A

FA Good evening. Welcome aboard.
May I see your boarding pass, please?

P Here you are. My seat is 30F.

FA Please take the other aisle. Your seat is in the back of the cabin.

P Thanks.

FA You're welcome, sir.

B

FA Good afternoon. Welcome aboard.
May I see your boarding pass, please?

P Here you are. it's 24A.

FA Thank you. your seat is in the middle of the cabin on your right.

P Thanks.

C

FA Good morning, Sir. welcome aboard.
May I see your boarding pass, please?

P It was checked a moment ago at the gate.

FA I'm sorry to bother you, but we must reconfirm the boarding pass according to aviation law.

P Here it is.

FA Your seat is 32H. please take the aisle on the left.

P Thanks.

Situation 2 Passenger with heavy hand carriers

• ***words and phrases***

store	coatroom
compartment	double-check
seat number	

FA: Flight Attendant | **P**: Passenger

A

FA	Good morning? May I help you with your bags?
P	Yes. Thanks.
FA	You're welcome. May I have your boarding pass, please?
P	Here you are.
FA	This way, please. Here is your seat. Would you mind keeping your bags under the seat in front of you?
P	Of course not.
FA	Thank you. If you need any assistance, please let us know.

B

FA This bag is too heavy to store in the overhead compartment and it's too big to store under the seat in front of you. if you don't mind, I will place it in the coatroom.

P Yes. When will I be able to get it back?

FA As soon as we land, I will return it to you. May I double-check your seat number?

(after arrival)

FA Thank you for waiting. here is your bag we stored in the coatroom for you.

P Thanks.

Situation 3 Mother with an infant

• *words and phrases*

baby bassinet	set up
i'll get one for you	during the flight
would you like a baby bassinet	diaper
formula	

FA: Flight Attendant | **P**: Passenger

A

FA Good afternoon? May I help you with your bags?

P Yes. Thank you.

FA You're welcome. May I see your boarding pass, please?

P Here you are.

FA This way, please. This is your seat. Would you like a baby bassinet?

P Yes, please.

FA I'll get one for you after take-off.

(after take-off)

FA Would you like me to set up the bassinet for you?

P Yes, please.

FA	We also have baby food, diapers and bottles. If you need anything during the flight, please let me know.
P	Thank you very much.

B

FA	Good morning, ma'am. I'm in charge of this section. we have some baby items such as diapers, baby food, baby formula and bottles. if you need anything, please let me know.
P	Yes. thank you.
FA	Would you like to have a bassinet for your baby?
P	Yes, please.
FA	I will set up a bassinet after take-off. Here is a plastic bag for the garbage during the flight.
P	Thank you so much.
FA	It's my pleasure, ma'am. Enjoy your flight.

Situation 4 UM(Unaccompanied Minor)

• *words and phrases*

draw	nervous
entertainment system	UM(unaccompanied Minor)

FA: Flight Attendant | **P**: Passenger

A

FA	Hi, I'm Ji Young. What's your name?
P	Hi, my name is Jennifer.
FA	Jennifer. That's a beautiful name. your seat is 15B. How old are you?
P	I'm seven years old.
FA	Do you like drawing pictures? We have a gift for you. You can draw pictures with it.
P	Thank you. Can I watch movies?
FA	Of course. You can watch movies on the screen and play games. Let me help you with your seatbelt. The flight time to Vancouver is 10 hours. Your meal will be ready 40 minutes after take-off. The first meal is chicken nugget and the second one is spaghetti. If you want to go to the toilet or need any of my assistance, please push this

button.

P Thanks.

B

FA Hello, I'm Eun Jin. I will be your guide today. what's your name?

P Hi, my name is Na Eun Kim.

FA Your seat is 31B right over here.

P I am a little nervous because I will be your guide today alone.

FA Don't worry. I will put your baggage in the overhead bin. let me take out some things you may need from your bag before putting it away.

P Please give me my color pencils and my notebook.

FA Sure. here they are.

P Thank you.

FA If you need any help, please push this button.

영국항공british airways

영국항공은 이코노미 클래스는 "월드 트레블러"world traveller, 비즈니스 클래스는 "클럽월드"club world 라는 이름으로 사용하고 있다. 타 항공사와 차별화된 클래스별 이름으로 브랜딩하고 있다.
클럽월드의 광고에서는 기내의 창문을 이용해 졸린 눈을 효과적으로 나타내며 편안하고 여유로운 좌석에서 휴식을 즐기며 여행하라는 의미를 재치있게 전달하고 있다.

2. Seating arrangement

Situation 1 Passenger standing in the aisle

• ***words and phrases***

safety
walking around
during boarding time

FA: Flight Attendant | **P**: Passenger

FA	Are you having trouble finding your seat?
P	No, I am just walking around.
FA	Well, would you please take your seat while others are boarding for your safety?
P	Oh, I will sit down.
FA	Thank you, sir. I would appreciate it.

Situation 2 Wrong seat

• ***words and phrases***

wrong seat	would you please ~?
I'm afraid	
behind	
change	

FA: Flight Attendant | **P1**: Passenger 1 | **P2**: Passenger 2

A

P1 Excuse me, Miss. I think this is my seat.

FA May I see your boarding pass, please?

……. Thank you, sir.

(to passenger 2)

Excuse me, ma'am. May I see your boarding pass, please?

……. Thank you, ma'am.

But I am afraid you are in the wrong seat.

Your seat is right behind this one.

Would you please move to the seat behind?

P2 Oh, I am sorry,

FA (to passenger 1)

Here you are, sir.

B

P1	Excuse me. I think this is my seat but someone is sitting in it.
FA	May I see your boarding pass, please? (to passenger2) Excuse me. can I see your boarding pass, please? I'm afraid you are in the wrong seat. Your seat is behind this one. Would you please move to your seat?
P2	Oh, really? I'm sorry. Where is my seat?
FA	This is your seat. Have a pleasant flight.
P2	Thanks.

Situation 3 Duplicated seat

• ***words and phrases***

duplicate	seating arrangement
rearrange	immediately

FA: Flight Attendant | **P1**: Passenger 1 | **P2**: Passenger 2

A

P1 Excuse me, Miss. This gentleman is sitting in my seat.

FA (to passenger 1)

May I see your boarding pass, please?

……. Thank you, sir.

(to passenger 2)

Excuse me, ma'am. May I see your boarding pass, please?

……. Thank you, ma'am.

(to both)

I am sorry. There has been some mistake with the seating arrangement.

(to passenger 1)

Come this way, please.

Please wait here for a few minutes, sir. while I

check this for you.

……. Thank you for waiting, sir.

Here is your modified boarding pass.

We are sorry for the inconvenience.

B

P1	Excuse me. Someone is sitting in my seat.
FA	May I see your boarding pass, please? I'm afraid that there has been a mistake in seating arrangements. Would you mind waiting here, sir? I will check it for you immediately.
P1	Sure.
	(after a while)
FA	thank you for waiting. Your seat has been rearranged. it's 35B. May I assist you to your seat? Here you are. I'm sorry for the inconvenience. Have a pleasant flight.
P1	Thanks.

Situation 4 Seats not together

• *words and phrases*

assigned	have a nice flight
occupied	thank you for your cooperation
across the aisle	would you mind changing seats
by the window	

FA: Flight Attendant | **P1**: Passenger 1 | **P2**: Passenger 2

A

P1	Excuse me, Miss. my wife and I are sitting separately. Are there any empty seats where we can sit together?
FA	I understand, sir. After take-off I will come back and let you know. (after check) I am sorry, sir. But all the seats are occupied today. Where is your wife sitting?
P1	Just across the aisle there.
FA	Alright, sir. Just a moment, please.

(to passenger 2 sitting next to passenger 1's wife)

Sir, this lady and her husband have been assigned seats apart and would like to sit together. Would you mind changing seats with her husband?

P2 I guess I do not mind. Where should I sit?

FA Thank you, sir. There is the seat right across the aisle, by the window. Come this way, please. Here we are.

Have a nice flight.

Thank you for your cooperation, sir.

B

FA Excuse me. my sisters are sitting over there, and we want to sit together.

P1 Is it possible that we can sit together?

FA I will see if I can help you after take-off, sir.

I'll be back soon and let you know.

P1 Thanks.

(after take-off)

FA Thank you for waiting. We have some seats available in the middle of the cabin, sir. Would that be alright?

P1 Yes, that would be great.

FA This way, please. Here are your seats have a nice flight.

타이항공thai airways

타이 국민 특유의 친절한 서비스로 정평이 난 타이항공의 슬로건인 "Smooth as Silk"비단결처럼 부드러운는 태국 전통 실크의 부드럽고 화려한 이미지에 부합하고자 하는 타이항공의 노력을 승객들에게 심어주고 있다.

Situation 5 Upgrade

• *words and phrases*

upgrade	section
empty	take care of

FA: Flight Attendant | **P**: Passenger

P Excuse me, Miss. I would like to sit in the first class cabin if there are any empty seats.

FA I am sorry, sir. We are not allowed to upgrade passengers' seating.

All seating arrangements must be taken care of before boarding.

3. Hand-carry baggage

Situation 1 Check hand-carry baggage

• ***words and phrases***

bring	boarding gate
hand-carry baggage	coatroom
overhead bin	belonging
groud staff	

FA: Flight Attendant | **P**: Passenger

A

FA Excuse me, sir. You have too much hand-carry baggage.
Every belonging must put under the seat in front of you or in the overhead bin.

P You mean I cannot bring all of these?

FA I am afraid not, sir. You will have to check in one of these with our ground staff outside the boarding gate.
I will keep the other bags here on board for you until you get back.
I am sorry for the inconvenience.

B

P	Excuse me, Miss. I can't find any places to store my bag.
FA	Oh, I'm so sorry. If you don't mind, I'll keep it in the coatroom in the front of the cabin. Is that allright with you?
P	Sure, thank you.
FA	You're welcome, sir. If you need anything during the flight, please let me know.
P	All right.

C

P	Excuse me. My bag doesn't fit under the seat and the overhead bin is full.
FA	Would you like me to keep your bag in the coatroom?
P	Could you do that? for me Thanks.
FA	It's my pleasure. Have a nice flight.

Situation 2 Handling baggage and coats

• ***words and phrases***

coat room	cooperation
keep	enjoyable

FA: Flight Attendant | **P**: Passenger

A

FA	Excuse me. Would you like me to keep your coat in the coat room?
P	Yes, please. Thanks.
FA	You're welcome. Have a pleasant flight.

B

FA	Excuse me. Would you like me to keep this for you in the coatroom?
P	No, thanks. I'll keep it here.
FA	All right. Have an enjoyable flight.

C

FA	Excuse me. Are these all your bags?
P	Yes, they are. is there any problem?
FA	I'm sorry but we have to keep the aisle clear at all times. Would you please put them in the overhead bin?
P	Oh, I see.
FA	I will help you. Thank you for your cooperation.

4. Pre-flight check for Take-off

Situation 1 Safety check

• ***words and phrases***

fasten	tray table
unfasten	window shade
airline regulation	electronic devices
seatback	upright position

FA: Flight Attendant | **P**: Passenger

■ *seat belt*

FA Excuse me. Would you mind fastening your seat belt, please?

P I don't like fastening the seat belt.

FA I'm sorry but I must ask you to fasten your seat belt for take-off. It's an airline regulation for your safety. After take-off when the fasten seat belt sign is off, you can unfasten your seat belt. Thank you for your cooperation.

▪ seat belt

FA	Would you please fasten your seatbelt?
P	Sure.
FA	And return your seatback to the upright position, please.
P	Oh, okay.
FA	Thank you, sir.

▪ tray table

FA	Excuse me, sir. Would you mind closing your tray table, please?
P	Alright.
FA	Thank you. you can use it again after take-off.
P	Okay.

▪ tray table

FA	Excuse me. Would you mind folding your tray table? We will be taking off shortly.
P	Okay.
FA	Thank you for your cooperation.

■ *window shade*

FA	Excuse me, could you please open your window shade?
P	Oh, the Sun is too bright for me.
FA	I'm sorry but for safety reasons, we have to keep them open during take-off and landing.
P	Okay.
FA	Thank you for your cooperation.

■ *electronic devices*

FA	Excuse me, sir. Is your cell phone set to flight mode?
P	I don't think so.
FA	You are allowed to use your electronic devices during the flight as long as they are set to flight mode.
P	Okay, I will.
FA	Thank you for your cooperation.

루프트한자Lufthansa

독일 루프트한자의 광고이다. 침대와 영화관 의자에 기내 세이프티safety 벨트를 올려놓은 것은 침대처럼 편안한 좌석, 영화관만큼 재미있는 즐길 거리가 있다는 것을 고객에게 보여주고 있다.

항공상식 9 엔진 2개로 태평양을 논스톱 횡단한다

엔진이 2개인 항공기로 태평양을 논스톱 횡단한다면 믿을 수 있을까? 서울서 미 서부인 로스앤젤레스나 샌프란시스코까지의 비행시간은 엔진이 4개인 B747-400의 경우, 평균 11시간 정도가 소요된다. 그러나 2개의 엔진만 가지고 있는 항공기가 이 긴 시간을 비행할 수 있으려면 승객이나 화물을 하나도 안 싣고 비행해야 하지만 그나마 엔진출력이 따라줘야 한다는 제한이 있다.

하지만 요즘은 엔진이 2개인 항공기들도 거뜬히 태평양을 10시간 이상씩 횡단한다. 바로 B777기와 B767기종이다. 그만큼 엔진 신뢰성이 높아졌다는 것이며 엔진 출력이 향상되었다는 것이다. B777의 경우 1개의 엔진 출력이 9만 파운드로, B747-400의 엔진 한 개의 출력이 5만 6천 파운드 정도에 비해 2배에 가깝다. 그렇다고 이 두 기종이 모두 태평양을 횡단할 수 있는 것은 아니다. 엔진이 2개인 항공기가 바다를 건너기 위해서는, 각국 정부로부터 쌍발항공기에 의한 장거리 운항ETOPSExtended Range Twin Engine Operation 허가를 항공사들이 받아야 한다.

ETOPS는 항공 운송용 쌍발 항공기가 운항 중에 1개의 엔진이 고장났을 때 다른 1개의 엔진으로 순항속도로 비행하여 착륙 가능한 공항으로부터 60분을 초과하는 지점을 포함하는 노선을 운항하는 것을 말한다.

미연방항공국FAA의 경우 ETOPS 최대 회항시간을 1985년에 120분, 1989년에 180분까지 인가하도록 규정을 제정했고 최근 지난 1월 말 B777에 대해207분으로 연장한 바 있다. ETOPS 규정에 의한 운항은 전 세계적으로 일상적이고 안전하며 고도로 성공적인 것으로 입증되고 있는 것이다. 대한항공의 경우 현재 B777에 대해 180분 ETOPS를 인가받고 있으며, 이 기종으로 서울서 샌프란시스코를 논스톱으로 연결하고 있다.

180분 ETOPS 운항은 엔진의 신뢰성이 비행 중 엔진 정지율이 5만 시간당 1회 이하여야 인가된다.

일반적으로 항공기가 대양을 횡단할 때 그냥 최단 거리를 비행하는 것으로 알고 있는데, 서울서 미국을 가는 항공로를 예로 들면 전부 대륙을 끼고 길이 나 있다. 바로 비행 중 엔진이 고장 났을 때 내릴 수 있는 대체공항을 염두에 두고 항공로가 만들어지기 때문이다.

TIPS FOR A COMFORTABLE AND CAREFREE FLIGHT

By Dr. Dalbir Singh Sagoo, Senior Aviation Medical Examiner

At Malaysia Airlines, we care for your safety and comfort. For your general inflight well-being, we would recommend the following.

- Be physically and mentally relaxed and enjoy the flight. Do some reading, talking, watch movies or take a nap.
- Wear comfortable clothes, suitable shoes and preferably tights or support stockings.
- Drink adequate water or fruit juices. Avoid too much caffeine and alcoholic beverages which may cause dehydration. Eat a lot of fruits and avoid food high in sodium and salt.
- Avoid prolonged sitting. Walk about when possible. Shake legs once in a while!
- Do the simple in-flight exercises illustrated on this page to exercise the foot, leg, hip and back muscles and improve blood circulation.
- Gentle massaging of the feet, legs, body and arms has beneficial effects.
- If you experience discomfort such as pain and swelling of your legs, rapid or difficulty in breathing, please seek immediate medical attention on arrival.

Have a pleasant flight!

BASIC EXERCISES FOR TRAVELLERS

- Raise your arms so that your elbows form a 90 degree angle at chest level. Press the palms of your hands together. Hold the position for six seconds, relax and repeat five to ten times.

- Sit with one foot flat on the floor close to your chair. Raise the opposite foot five inches off the floor, first flexing and then pointing your toes. This increases circulation in your lower leg and foot muscles. Repeat up to 20 times. Do the same with the other foot.

- Tilt your head backwards, arch your back and hold for six seconds, then bring your chin down to rest on your chest. Hold for six seconds, then repeat five to ten times.

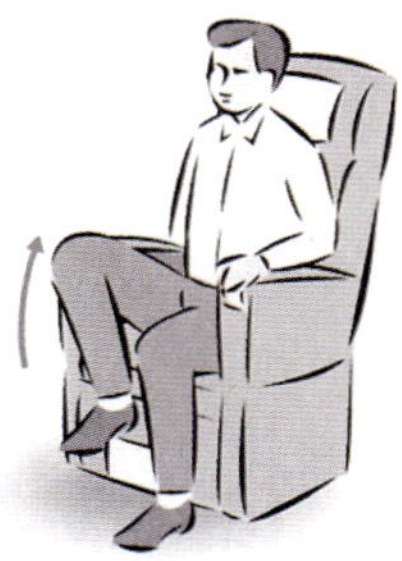

- Sit upright on the edge of the couch or chair with your back straight, lift one foot and then the other as if you are marching, bringing your knees high and pumping your arms as you go. Maintain exercise as long as you are comfortable.

- Press both elbows against the seat while keeping your head and chest up and chin in. Breathe normally, hold the contraction for six seconds, then relax. Repeat five times.

Unit 3

In-flight service

Situation 1 Earphone

• *words and phrases*

charge	it's free of charge
would you care for	may I take

FA: Flight Attendant | **P**: Passenger

A

FA	Excuse me. Would you care for an earphone?
P	Do you charge for it?
FA	No, ma'am. It's complimentary.
P	I will have one.
FA	Here it is. Enjoy your flight.

B

FA	Here is your headphone, sir.
P	Thank you. where can I plug it in?
FA	Right here, on the armrest.

P Thank you.

FA It's my pleasure. Please feel free to ask me if you need any help.

P Okay.

아비앙카 항공avianca

커피로 유명한 콜롬비아의 항공사 아비앙카는 커피잔과 라테아트로 흥미로운 광고를 선보였다. 라테아트로는 아비앙카의 탁월한 비행과 서비스를 적절히 표현하고 있으며, 커피잔 손잡이를 이용해서는 상파울루에서 보고타로 향하는 항공기 출발 및 도착 시간을 보여 주고 있다.

Situation 2 Towel service

• *words and phrases*

distribution	pick up
be careful	would you care for

FA: Flight Attendant | **P**: Passenger

distribution

FA Would you care for a hot towel?

P Yes, please.

FA Please be careful. It's hot.

P Thank you.

towel pick up

FA Excuse me. May I take your towel?

P Yes. Thank you.

FA You're welcome.

Situation 3 Offering drinks

• *words and phrases*

would you like something to drink	mixers
on the rock	enjoy your drink
neat	soft drinks
liquors	refill

FA: Flight Attendant | **P**: Passenger

■ (*non alcoholic drinks*) - *juice*

FA	Would you like something to drink?
P	Yes. What kind of juice do you have?
FA	We have orange juice, apple juice and tomato juice.
P	I would like to have apple juice.
FA	Certainly, sir. Here is your juice. Enjoy your drink.
P	Thanks.

■ (*non alcoholic drinks*) - *tea or coffee*

FA	Would you care for something to drink?
P	Yes, I'd like to have a cup of coffee.
FA	How would you like your coffee?

P With cream, please.

FA Certainly, ma'am. Here's your coffee with cream. It's hot.

please be careful.

P Thank you.

alcoholic drinks

FA Excuse me, sir. Would you care for something to drink?

P May I have a glass of whiskey?

FA On the rocks? Or neat?

P whiskey on the rocks please.

FA Sure. Enjoy your drink.

P Thanks.

alcoholic drinks

FA May I get you a drink?

We have juices, soft drinks, beers and alcoholic beverage.

P I'll have a Cass, please.

FA I'm sorry but I'm afraid we don't have Cass on this flight.

P Then what kind of beer do you have?

FA We have a selection of Heineken, Hite and Budwiser.

P Heineken, please.

FA Sure. Here's your beer. Enjoy your drink.

P Thanks.

▪ *cocktail request*

FA What would you like to drink?

P Is it possible for me to have a Bloody Mary?

FA Yes, of course. We can make many kinds of cocktail with the liquors and mixers we have.

P Oh, very good. One Bloody Mary, please.

▪ *serving wine*

FA Would you like some wine with your meal?

P What kind of wine do you have?

FA We have red, white and sparkling wine.

P I'd like a glass of white wine. Do you have chardonnay?

FA I'm sorry but we only have sauvignon blanc and Riesling.

P Ok. I will have a glass of Riesling, Please.

FA Certainly. This wine was produced in Germany in 2004.

P	Thank you.

refill

P	Excuse me. Can I have another drink?
FA	Sure. What would you care for, ma'am?
P	Another beer, please.
FA	I'll get one for you soon.
	Here is your beer. Enjoy your drink.
P	Thank you.

collection

FA	Excuse me, may I take your glass?
P	Yes, please.
FA	Thank you, sir.

Situation 4 Spilled drink on a passenger

• *words and phrases*

wipe up	manage
accept	may I help you
apology	never mind

FA: Flight Attendant | **P**: Passenger

FA	I'm terribly sorry, sir. Let me get something to wipe it off. May I help you wipe it off?
P	No, that's fine. I can manage it.
FA	Please accept my apology.
P	That's okay.
FA	I am sorry again, sir.

에어프랑스air france

2004년 에어프랑스는 네덜란드에 기반을 둔 KLM 네덜란드 항공과 합병하여 유럽 최대의 항공사로 재탄생하였다. 허브공항은 파리의 샤를르 드골 공항이다.

에어프랑스의 퍼스트클래스인 La Premiere 객실에서는 세계적인 미슐랭 스타 셰프 "기마르탱" 등이 만든 요리를 맛볼 수 있다. 또한 새로운 기내식을 제공하기 위해 두 달마다 기내식 메뉴를 바꾸고 있다.

Situation 5 Meal service

• *words and phrases*

meal	choice
serving	go well with
breakfast	enjoy your meal
load	right away
dinner	request
would you mind ~?	offer

FA: Flight Attendant | **P**: Passenger

serving breakfast

FA Excuse me, sir. Would you mind opening your tray table?
We're serving breakfast now. We have omelet and green tea congee.

P I'll have an omelet.

FA Would you like some coffee or juice?

P I would like to have coffee please.

FA Certainly. Enjoy your meal.

P Thanks.

serving dinner

P	What's the meal today?
FA	We have bibimbap with (rice and vegetable).
P	The bibimbap sounds nice. I would like to try it
FA	Sure. Would you like to have something to drink with the meal?
P	Which drink would go well with the bibimbap?
FA	White wine goes better with bibimbap.
P	Okay, I'll have some white wine, please.
FA	Enjoy your meal.
P	Thank you.

serving special meal-kosher

FA	Excuse me. Are you Mrs. Grace who requested a kosher meal?
P	Yes, that's me.
FA	I need to heat them before serving. Would you please open the meal?
P	OK. I'll open the plastic bags.
FA	Would you like something to drink before dinner?
P	The drink in the box is enough. Thanks.

special meal-not loaded

P Excuse me. I requested a Muslim meal when I made my reservation.

FA I'm sorry, ma'am. May I have your name, please?

P My name is Mary Albert.

FA Thanks. I will check your meal immediately.
I'm so sorry ma'am. Your meal wasn't loaded.
May I offer another choice? would you care for beef with rice?

P Well, all right.

FA I'll get one for you right away.
Here is your meal. I'm sorry for the inconvenience.
I hope you enjoy your meal.

Entr'ee run out

FA Excuse me, ma'am. We had a choice of beef and chicken but I'm afraid we've run out of the beef today.
we only have chicken left. Would that be alright with you?

P Alright. I'll take it.

FA Thank you for your understanding. I hope you enjoy your meal.

hot beverage service after meal service

FA	Would you care for some coffee?
P	Yes, please.
FA	Could you please put your cup on this tray? thank you. Here is your coffee. Please be careful. it's very hot. Would you like some cream and sugar with your coffee?
P	No, thanks.
FA	Enjoy your coffee.

meal tray collecting

FA	Excuse me. Are you finished with your meal?
P	Yes, I am.
FA	Thanks. may I take your tray?
P	Yes, please.
FA	Thank you.

대한항공korean air

항공사에서는 부가 수입을 창출할 수 있으며 또한 승객의 편리한 쇼핑을 위해 기내 면세품 판매를 하고 있다. 기내 면세품판매는 고객 입장에서는 목적지까지의 비행 중 편안하게 쇼핑을 할 수 있다는 장점이 있다.

Situation 6 In–flight duty–free

• *words and phrases*

duty-free	refund
purchase	currency
allow	liquor
instead	allowance
accept	change

FA: Flight Attendant | **P**: Passenger

selling duty-free items

FA Would you like to buy any duty-free item?

P What kind of whiskey do you have?

FA This shopping magazine has all the information about our duty-free sales.

P Do you know how much whiskey I can take into Singapore?

FA You are allowed one liter of liquor.

P OK. I'll have two bottles of whiskey.

FA How would you like to pay?

P I'll pay with credit card.

FA Certainly, Sir. I'll get your order.

(selling duty-free items) - item is sold out

P	Excuse me. I would like to buy one bobby brown eye shadow.
FA	I'm afraid it has sold out. Would you care for a Estee Lauder eye shadow, instead?
P	No thanks.
FA	I'm sorry for the inconvenience.

unacceptable currency

P	I'd like to buy three boxes of Korean red chili Paste. Can I pay in Canadian dollars?
FA	I'm afraid we do not accept Canadian dollars.
P	Can I pay by credit card?
FA	Certainly, sir. That will be 35 US dollars.
P	Here is my credit card.
FA	Could I have your signature, please?
P	Sure.
FA	Here is your receipt. thank you, sir.

refund

P	Excuse me, can I get a refund on these perfumes?
FA	Of course. let me have the receipt, please.

P	Here you go.
FA	Thank you. just a moment, please. May I have the perfumes? Here's your refund receipt ma'am.
P	Thank you.
FA	You're welcome.

duty free allowance

P	Excuse me. Do you know how much perfume I can take into Cebu?
FA	This book will show you the duty free allowance for Cebu. You may take up to 80 milliliters of perfume.
P	Oh, I see. Thanks.
FA	You're welcome.

Situation 7 Entry documents

• *words and phrases*

disembarkation card	arrival card
embarkation	complete
custom declaration card	transit
resident	e-passport
fill out	ESTA
immigrant	

FA: Flight Attendant | **P**: Passenger

▪ *disembarkation card*

P Excuse me. I'll be staying in Korea for 15 days. Do I need to fill out disembarkation card?

FA Yes. Foreigners entering Korea must fill out the card.
Would you like me to help you with it?

P No thanks.

▪ *transit passengers*

P Excuse me. I will be at Incheon only for a few hours and then I will be flying on to Osaka. Do I need this card?

FA	No sir. You don't need to fill out the card.
P	Alright.

▪ *customs declaration card*

P	Excuse me. Will I need customs declaration card for Korea?
FA	All passengers must fill out both side of the card. Would like me to help you?
P	No thanks.

▪ *entering the United States*

FA	Is the USA your final destination?
P	Yes.
FA	Are you a US citizen, a US resident, a US immigrant visa holder?
P	No, I'm a Korean tourist.
FA	Do you have a US entry visa?
P	No, I have an e-passport and ESTA.
FA	Then you have to fill in an I-94W form as well as a customs form. You only need to fill in one customs form per family.
P	All right. Thank you.

immigrant

P	Excuse me. I live in the USA, but I'm not a citizen yet. Do I need to fill out this card.
FA	May I ask whether you have an immigrant visa?
P	Yes, I have an immigrant visa.
FA	Then you only have to fill out the customs declaration form.
P	Thanks.

Situation 8 Preparation for landing

• ***words and phrases***

return	clear
on board	upright
shortly	in front of
landing	continue
return the seat back to the upright position	

FA: Flight Attendant | **P**: Passenger

■ *earphone collection*

FA Excuse me, ma'am. May I have your earphone, please?
We will be landing shortly. Thank you ma'am.

P I'm still watching the movie.

FA If you are still using them, you may continue to do so.

P Thank you.

FA You're welcome, sir.

■ *earphone collection*

FA Excuse me, sir. May I have your earphone, please?
We will be landing soon. thank you, sir.

	Did you have a nice flight?
P	Yes I did.
FA	I'm glad to hear that.

■ *safety check*

FA	Excuse me, sir. Would you please fasten your seatbelt and return your seatback to the upright position? We will be landing soon.
P	Alright.
FA	And open your window shade, please.
P	Yes, I will.
FA	Thank you, sir. Did you enjoy the flight?
P	Yes, I did.
FA	I am glad to hear that.

■ *collecting cups*

FA	Excuse me ma'am. Have you finished with your drink?
P	Yes, I have.
FA	May I take your cup?
P	Sure.
FA	We will be landing soon. Would you mind closing your tray table?

P O.K.

baggage check

FA Excuse me. Would you please put your bag in the overhead bin or under the seat in front of you? We will be landing shortly.

P Okay. I see.

FA Thank you.

baggage check

FA Excuse me. Is this your bag, ma'am?

P Yes.

FA I'm sorry but we have to keep the aisle clear for landing.
Would you mind keeping it under your seat?

P I will do that.

FA Thank you.

항공용어

DEFINITION OF COMMON AIR TRANSPORT TERMS

A

ADD 이미 예약된 사항에 추가하여 예약하는 것

Adult Fare 만 12세 이상 승객에게 적용되는 항공요금

Agency Commission 대리점이 판매한 여행자의 항공권이나 화물의 판매에 대하여 항공사에서 지불되는 소정의 수수료

Altitude 고도

Accompanied Minor 동반된 어린이

Attendant 동반자

Aisle Side 통로편의 좌석(Aisle Seat)

Alternative Airport 교체공항

B

Baby Bassine 기내용의 유아요람, 항공기 객실 앞의 벽면에 설치하여 사용하는 것

Baggage 여행자가 관광할 때 소지한 짐으로써 Checked Baggage와 Unchecked Baggage가 있다.

Baggage Claim Tag 수하물 증표

Boarding Pass 탑승권

Block Time 출발지의 주기장을 출발하여 목적지의 주기장에 도착하기까지의 시간

C

Cabin Crew 기내 승무원

Call Button 승객들이 승무원을 호출하는 버튼

Captain 기장

Catering 항공기에 식품류를 조달 및 탑재하는 것

Cockpit 조종실

Cockpit Crew 운항승무원, 항공기의 운항을 책임지고 있는 기장, 부조종사, 항법사로 구분된다.

Configuration 객실 내의 좌석배치를 말함

Control Tower 비행장 관제탑

Cancellation Charge 예약된 좌석을 사용하지 아니한 것에 대하여 부가되는 요금

Checked Baggage 여행자가 항공여행 시 부치는 짐. 여행자가 항공기 내에 들고 들어가는 것은 Hand Carry Baggage라고 한다.

Check-in 탑승수속

Child Fare 만 2세 이상 12세 미만 여행자에게 적용되는 항공요금

C.I.Q Customs, Immigration, Quarantine(세관, 출입국 심사, 검역)의 약자로 출국, 또는 입국 시 공항에서 관할관서가 행사는 check의 대상항목이다.

Circle Trip 출발지와 도착지가 동일지점으로 항로가 중복되지 않고 돌아오는 일주 관광

Connection Time 연결 항공편으로 갈아타는데 필요한 시간

Charter Flight 대절 항공기, 전세 항공기

Cabin Service 기내에서의 각종 Service

Connection Time Interval 최소 연결 필요시간(Minimum Connecting Time)은 각 공항마다 다르므로 관광일정 작성 시 유의하여야 한다.

Confirmation 예약의 확인

D

Destination 최종목적지

Double Booking 중복 예약

Downgrade 등급의 변경, 상위에서 하위등급으로 변경하는 것(1등석 → 2등석 → 일반석)

DSR Daily Sales Report의 약어로서 항공권 판매에 관한 일일판매보고서

Duplicate Reservation 중복예약

Deplane Point 항공기에서 내리는 지점(공항)

Divert 항공기가 기상 및 제반 여건에 의해 예정 공항에 착륙하지 못하고 인근의 다른 공항에 착륙하는 것

Divide 여러 명의 여행자가 예약되어 있는 경우 그 가운데 한 명 또는 다수를 분리해 내는 것

Deportee 추방자

Deposit 예치금

Direct Flight 직행편

E

Economy Class(EY) 일반석

Economy Fare Economy Class 요금

Embarkation Disembarkation Card 출입국 기록 카드

Endorsement 항공권의 지정된 탑승구간을 다른 항공사로 양도하는 것

Estimated Time of Arrival(ETA) 예정 도착시간

Estimated Time of Departure(ETD) 예정 출발시간

Excess Baggage 무료 수하물 허용량을 초과한 수하물로서 일정금액을 지불하여야 한다.

Excess Baggage Charge 초과 수하물 운송을 위한 요금

F

Fare 운임

First Class 일등실

Flag Carrier(National Carrier) 일국을 대표하는 항공사 대한항공은 한국의 Flag Carrier라 할 수 있다.

Flight Coupon 항공권의 일부로서 여행자가 탑승수속 시 공항에서 탑승권과

교환한다.

Free Baggage Allowance 무료 수하물, 즉 지불을 받지 않고 운송되는 일정량의 수하물, 일반적으로 FC요금 지불 여행자는 30kg, EY요금 지불 여행자는 20kg, 태평양 노선은 2개의(짐 한 개당 32kg까지 가능) 짐을 무료로 운송할 수 있다.

Forced Landing 비상착륙, 기체구조상의 고장, 악천후, 연료결여 등의 원인 때문에 계속 비행이 허락지 않았을 때에 행하는 불시착을 말함

Flight Rules 비행규정

G

Galley 항공기내의 주방

Gateway(Gateway City) 어느 지역에의 문호로 되어 있는 도시, 미국 해안의 문호도시는 Seattle, San Francisco 및 Los Angeles 등

Go Show Passenger(Stand By) 만석, 혹은 요금상의 제한 등에 의하여 예약할 수 없는 여행자가 좌석이 생기면 탑승하려고 공항까지 와서 탑승을 기다리는 것

General Sales Agent(GSA) 총 판매 대리점

Government Transportation Request(GTR) 정부가 정부기관관련 직원의 공용여행 시 발행하는 항공권 요청서

H

Home Port Flight 거주지로의 비행

Hand Carry Baggage 기내에 가지고 들어갈 수 있는 수하물, 부피와 수량에 제한이 있다.

Hanger 항공기의 격납고 또는 기내의 양복걸이 캐비넷

I

IATA International Air Transport Association의 약어로서 1945년 4월에 아바나에서 결성되었다.

ICAO International Civil Aviation Organization의 약어로 국제 민간항공협정에 의하여 1947년 설립된 국제민간항공기구. 본부의 소재지는 캐나다의 몬트리올, 가맹국은 141개국이며, 한국은 1952년 12월 11일 가입하였다.

Immigration 법무부 출입국심사

Infant Fare 유아요금. 국제선에서는 2세 미만으로서 좌석을 확보하지 않을 때에는 보통요금의 10%, 확보할 때에는 어린이 요금(Child Fare)을 지불하여야 한다. 국내선에서는 만 3세 미만은 무료이다.

Itinerary Change 여행일정의 변경

Inbound(Incoming) 외국에서 국내로의 여행

Inflight Movie 기내용 영화

Interpreter 통역 승무원

L

Landing Gear 착륙장치

Late Cancellation 항공사가 정한 일정시간 이후의 예약 취소

Late Show Passenger 탑승수속(Check-in) 마감 후에 탑승수속 Counter에 나타나는 여행자

Load Factor 여행자 또는 화물의 탑재 가능량에 대하여 실제로 탑재한 여행자 또는 화물의 탑승률 또는 탑재율을 말함

Local Time 현지시간

M

Maintenance 정비

MAS 공항에서의 Meet and Assistance Service, VIP 또는 특별취급이 필요한

여행자에 대한 서비스

Miscellaneous Charge Order(MCO) 항공사나 대리점이 발행한 MCO에 기재된 사람에게 적절한 Ticket발급이나 Service의 제공을 요청하는 서류이다. 요금이나 초과 수하물 운임의 지불 혹은 차액 등의 완불을 위한 지불수단으로서 이용되고 있다.

Minimum Connection Time 최소 연결편 탑승시간

Mis-Connection 항공기를 바꾸어 탑승할 때 접속지점까지 수송하는 항공편이 지연되거나 결항하여 탑승하지 못하는 것을 말함

N

Non Revenue Passenger 무임탑승 여행자. 무료로 여행할 수 있도록 계약된 사람들로서 대부분이 항공사 직원들이다.

No Record(NOREC) 여행자가 탑승 수속 시 예약된 Ticket을 제시했으나 항공사 쪽에는 예약을 받은 기록이나 좌석을 확인해준 근거가 없는 상태를 말함

Normal Fare 정상 요금

No Show(NOSHO) Mis-Connection 이외의 이유로서, 여행자가 예약 취소를 하지 않은 채로 예약편에 탑승하지 않는 것

No Subject To Load(NOSUB) 무상 혹은 할인요금을 지불하나 여행자가 일반 유료여행자와 같이 좌석 예약을 할 수 있도록 하는 것

O

Out Port Flight 거주지에서 다른 목적지로의 비행

On-Line / Off-Line On-Line은 항공사가 정기 운행되고 있는 것을, Off-Line은 반대로 항공기가 정기적으로 운항되고 있지 않은 것을 말한다.

Open Ticket 예약이 되어있지 않는 항공권을 말함

Over Booking 어떤 비행편에 판매 가능한 좌석수보다 많은 여행자의 예약을 접수한 상태

Over Riding Commission 통상의 대리점 수수료에 가산하여 지불되는 추가 수수료

Outbound 자국을 기준으로 국외로의 여행

Over-Weight Baggage 초과 수하물

Over Collection 초과 징수금

Operation 운항

P

Passenger(PAX) 항공 승객

Passenger Coupon 국제선 항공권의 최종 Page의 쿠폰, 승객 쿠폰

Passenger Service Coupon 통과 승객들에게 공항에서 식사나 음료 등을 제공하기 위한 쿠폰

Prepaid Ticket Advice(PTA) 항공요금의 선불제도로서 요금 지불인이 멀리 떨어져 있는 여행자를 위하여 요금을 불입하고 실제로 탑승할 승객이 있는 곳에서 발권하여 탑승여행자에게 항공권을 전해주도록 통지하는 것

Published Fare 요금표에 공시되어 있는 공표 요금을 말함

Q

Quarantine 검역

R

Ramp 항공기 계류장

Reconfirmation 좌석예약의 재확인

Reissue 항공권의 재발행

Refueling 연료 재급유

Refund Ticket의 미상용분에 대한 금액을 구매자에게 환불해 주는 것

Rerouting 항공권에 기재된 탑승예정의 경로를 변경하는 것

Reservation 예약

Round Trip 왕복관광

Runway 활주로

S

Special Fare 특별요금

Stand By 여분의 좌석이 발생했을 때 좌석을 배정 받게 되는 승객을 의미한다.

Stopover 도중체류 승객이 항공사와의 사전 예약하에 출발지와 목적지의 중간 기착지에서 체류하는 것

SUBLO(Subject To Load) 사전의 예약이 인정되지 않고 여석이 있을 때 탑승할 수 있는 제도. 무상 혹은 할인요금으로 탑승하는 승객 또는 항공사 직원 등이 적용됨

Special Meal 유아 등 특별음식을 요구하는 승객을 위한 식사

T

Tail Wind 뒤에서 불어오는 바람

Take Off 이륙

Taxiway 유도로. 공항에 있어서 Apron에서 활주로로 항공기가 이동하기 위하여 사용하는 길을 말함

Transit Passenger 타국에로의 통과목적만으로 입국하는 통과 여행자

Transit Without Visa(TWOV) 무사증 단기 체류의 준말이며 여행자이 규정된 조건하에서 입국사증 없이 어느 나라에 입국하여 짧은 기간 동안 체류할 수 있는 편의를 말한다.

U

Unaccompanied Minor(UM) 통상 UM이라 하며 3개월 이상 12세 미만의 유아나 어린이로 성인 보호자가 동반치 않고 단독 여행을 하는 경우

저/자/소/개

조인환Cho, Inhwan

세종대학교 호텔관광경영학과 및 동 관광대학원 겸임교수를 역임하였으며, 현재는 백석예술대학교 항공서비스학부 교수 겸 백석대학교 관광아카데미 교수로 재직 중이다.

미국 노스웨스트항공northwest airlines에서 Marketing Manager로 미국항공사연합u.s airline alliance에서 Marketing Director로 근무하였으며, 관심분야는 항공서비스마케팅, 항공사 전략적 제휴, 항공전자상거래 등이다.

정혜련Jung, Hyelyun

에미레이트항공emirates airlines에서 객실승무원cabin crew으로 근무하였다. 광주여자대학교 스튜어디스학과와 수원여자대학교 사회실무학과, 백석예술대학교 관광학부 겸임교수를 역임하였으며, 현재는 백석문화대학교 항공서비스전공 교수로 재직 중이다. 관심분야는 항공서비스경영, 글로벌 커뮤니케이션이다.

김은혜Kim, Eunhye

에어아시아airasia, 에티하드항공etihad airlines, 알리탈리아항공alitalia airlines에서 객실승무원cabin crew으로 근무하였으며, 핀에어, 걸프항공, 에티오피아항공 등 외국항공사 객실승무원 1차 면접관으로 활동하였다.

두원공과대학교 항공서비스학과, 서울문화예술대학교 항공서비스학과에서 외래교수로 재직하였으며, 현재는 백석예술대학교 항공서비스학부에서 겸임교수로 재직 중이다.

황유리Hwang, Yuri

에미레이트항공emirates airlines, 네덜란드항공KLM royal dutch airlines, 알리탈리아항공alitalia airlines에서 객실승무원으로 근무하였으며 상지영서대학교 항공서비스학과와 서정대학교 호텔경영과 외래강사를 역임하였으며, 현재는 백석예술대학교 항공서비스학부 겸임교수로 재직 중이다. 경희대학교 호텔관광대학 박사과정 중이며 관심분야는 서비스경영과 스마트관광이다.

저자와의
합의하에
인지첩부
생략

Airline Service English

2022년 8월 10일 초판 1쇄 인쇄
2022년 8월 15일 초판 1쇄 발행

지은이 조인환 · 정혜련 · 김은혜 · 황유리
펴낸이 진욱상
펴낸곳 백산출판사
교 정 박시내
본문디자인 이문희
표지디자인 오정은

등 록 1974년 1월 9일 제406-1974-000001호
주 소 경기도 파주시 회동길 370(백산빌딩 3층)
전 화 02-914-1621(代)
팩 스 031-955-9911
이메일 edit@ibaeksan.kr
홈페이지 www.ibaeksan.kr

ISBN 979-11-6639-249-8 93740
값 25,000원